Introduction

In the faces of Richard Fisher and his father, David, I could see the pain of hundreds of patients and their families who have passed through my office through the years.

Memory loss is never easy because there are no easy answers. There are no medical miracles I can offer such patients, no matter how much I might wish I could. My helplessness against the ravages of mental decline is the greatest failure of almost 25 years of practice as a neurologist.

Richard Fisher cleared his throat and looked at his hands clasped in his lap before he looked up at me and blurted, "I think Dad is having some problems with his memory."

"Can you give me a few details?" I asked.

"Sure," Richard answered, consulting a list he had brought with him. "Let's see, last week the electricity was turned off at the house because he hadn't paid the electric bill. When I checked the mailbox, it was overflowing with mail that he had forgotten to bring in. Yesterday, he flew into a rage and threw his water glass because he couldn't find his shoes. And on Tuesday, he got lost coming home from the drugstore. Do you want more?"

Richard leaned over and whispered, "I'm thinking I may need to take away his car keys."

Unfortunately, Mr. Fisher showed the classic signs of cognitive decline in aging commonly known as dementia.

I took a long look at David Fisher. The white-haired, kind-faced, 85-year-old man was patiently examining a painting on my office wall.

He startled a bit when I addressed him. "Mr. Fisher, how do you feel?"

"I feel fine," he answered amiably.

"Do you know what year this is?" I asked him.

Mr. Fisher hesitated a moment and then replied, "I'm not sure. I haven't checked the calendar."

That pretty much cinched it. That question comprises the simplest diagnostic test I have, but it's also one of the most definitive. Mr. Fisher was suffering from serious cognitive impairment. While the signs of David Fisher's serious impairment had been recent, I could tell there had been a gradual decline that was less noticeable.

It was once called senility, which maybe sounds a little kinder than our more modern term: dementia or Alzheimer's disease (AD).

"Aren't there some new drugs that can stop this?" asked Richard.

How many times I've been asked this question and how many times I have wished I could give them the answer they are so desperately seeking!

I lightly touched Richard on the shoulder, offering a tiny bit of comfort. "Yes, there are some drugs, but they have little real effect when the dementia is more advanced. I'm so sorry to tell you there is little that medical science can do to slow or reverse this decline," I told him as gently as I could.

I let the idea sink in. Richard's father was still alive and his body would likely live on for quite some time, given David Fisher's apparent good physical health. But the man Richard had known and loved all his life was fading from him. His mind would be gone long before his body was, putting a painful burden on his family.

The only good part of dementia is the patient's blessed lack of recognition of his situation.

Those who suffer the most are the family members who will watch a loved one fade away while they remain burdened with the emotional aspects of caring for a person who is only a shell, plus the onerous task of the physical care of an adult who may be far less than cooperative (and may even be combative), as well as the financial devastation that can accompany the need for long-term care.

It breaks my heart to see them bow and sometimes break under the weight of their love for one who is lost.

That first visit was too early to tell Richard Fisher about this. This was the time to sympathize with him and to mourn with him.

Two months later, Richard returned. He brought David with him and his wife, Marla, his teenaged daughter, Amy, and his mother, Rachel. The strain was already showing. There were worry lines on Richard's forehead. Rachel had an air of quiet desperation about her. Marla wrung her hands continuously and Amy alternated between teenage ennui and agitation.

I felt like I knew the Fishers far better than I actually did because they were so similar to so many families I have known in my decades of practice. My heart breaks a little bit more each time I have to tell a family that their loved one has begun a long journey into oblivion.

"We've decided to move Mom and Dad in with us," Richard announced, glancing at Marla and Amy for confirmation.

They all nodded grimly.

"How do you feel about that, Rachel?" I asked the frail elderly lady. I could tell she once had a backbone of steel, but her shoulders now slumped, a sign I had begun to interpret as the posture of someone carrying the weight of the world on her shoulders.

She looked at David for a long moment and then turned to me with tears in her eyes. "I don't think there is anything else I can do. I hate to admit it, but I can't do this by myself," she said quietly.

"And David, how do you feel about moving in with Richard and Marla?" I asked the patient.

"It'll be fun," David smiled. "I can play with the grandchildren every day."

Everyone laughed and Amy rolled her eyes in typical teenage fashion.

Memory Loss Is Not Inevitable
Secret Ways To Naturally Save Your Brain

by

Allen S. Josephs, M.D.

CommonSense
PUBLISHING

Table of Contents

That broke the tension, at least for the moment.

Richard turned to me when the others broke into nervous chatter. He clasped my arm.

"Dr. Josephs, please tell me that I can prevent this terrible memory loss from happening to me and the rest of my family!"

My gloom lifted.

Yes, this was something I could do. I could offer Richard and his family some hope.

I turned to Richard and smiled. "Yes, there is a great deal you can do in terms of prevention. I can help you with this."

Allen S. Josephs, M.D.
Livingston, N.J.

Acknowledgments

I would first like to acknowledge Ms. Kathleen Barnes who helped to edit this book. This is my second project with Kathleen. She is consistently professional and knowledgeable and an absolute pleasure to work with.

I would also like to pay tribute to my soul mate, Marlene, who has been my driving force and inspiration.

Finally, I must take off my hat for the literally tens of millions of caregivers of loved ones suffering with Alzheimer's and other dementing illnesses. Their dedication is truly amazing, and I hope this book provides them with some degree of comfort.

Is Memory Loss Inevitable As We Age?

We've all had those "moments." You know the ones I mean: you walk into a room to get something and can't remember why you're there, or you lose your car in the parking lot at the mall or you forget your best friend's name when you're getting ready to introduce him at a business function.

We usually laugh off these embarrassing moments, but somewhere in the back of our brains is a nagging fear: "Am I starting to lose my mind?" we ask ourselves. "Is this the beginning of the end?"

These moments are particularly distressing if we've watched a parent or grandparent or other loved one slide down into the abyss of Alzheimer's disease or other forms of dementia.

I think most of us fear losing our cognitive function more than we fear death.

THE UP SIDE

Memory loss, for most people, is not inevitable. Assuming you don't have any strong genetic risks for dementia and that you use your mind and eat a healthy diet, you can keep your brain healthy and your memory intact throughout your life.

Think of octogenarians, nonagenarians and even centenarians who have continued to make a contribution to our world in their old age.

Think of George Burns, the beloved comedian and actor who re-launched his career when he was in his 90s and who continued to delight audiences, delivering his lines with impeccable timing and wit until his death at the age of 100. And remember his compatriot, the legendary Bob Hope, who also lived to be 100 and continued to entertain U.S. troops until he was nearly 90. Remember, too, the incomparable actress Katharine Hepburn who was still making movies at the age of 87, winning Oscars into her late 70s: she lived to be 96.

Think of former president Gerald Ford, who died at the age of 93 and was actively giving policy advice well into his 90s. And then there was the curmudgeonly Sen. Strom Thurmond of South Carolina, the oldest senator in history, who held on to his seat in the U.S. Senate until his death at the age of 100.

Think of Marie Rudisill, whose witty and razor-sharp comments as the "Fruitcake Lady" on the Jay Leno show tickled millions of funny bones until her death at the age of 95.

The list goes on and on: Mother Teresa, tirelessly fulfilling her mission in life until her death at 87; Nelson Mandela, the South African who ushered his country into a new era of equality, still doing likewise at the age of 89 despite the physical hardships that resulted from his long imprisonment; Max Planck, the father of quantum physics, who was still giving lectures a few months before his death at the age of 89; and George Bernard Shaw, who died after a fall from a ladder at the age of 94 and was at work on another play at the time of his death.

Certainly it's obvious that it is possible to remain mentally alert and inquisitive, to learn new things and to engage in social interactions into extreme old age.

But I don't think that it's an easy task to hang on to all your marbles late in life.

It is possible to remain mentally alert and inquisitive, to learn new things and to engage in social interactions into extreme old age, but you'll have to work at it.

If you think of the famous people I mentioned who maintained full, rich and cognitive lives well into their 80s and 90s and even beyond, you'll see some common threads:

1. All of them, without exception, are and were mentally active. There's not a single couch potato in this lot! They consciously sought new ideas, new experiences and new challenges. They discussed ideas and circled them from many viewpoints. They literally exercised their brains, so their brains "stayed in shape," and remained flexible and strong.

2. Their activities involved a great deal of social interaction. Researchers tell us that a social network and the challenges of social interaction go a long way toward preserving mental function, whether it is attending a regular bridge club meeting or a serving on the board of directors of your favorite charity, delivering meals on wheels or simply getting together regularly with friends and family.

3. They continued to work in at least some capacity, adding to the challenges to their brains.

4. They moved their bodies. No, none of them were running marathons or winning bodybuilding competitions, but they were clearly far from chair- or couch-bound. Whether it's walking, gardening, taking care of a house or riding a bike, the effect is the same: the simple movements of day-to-day living help preserve brain function. In fact, Nelson Mandela still works out in his home gym for an hour every morning—even at the age of 89!

Until the last 15 years or so, scientists believed the brain could not grow new cells and that we die with the same number of brain cells with which we were born.

But in the early 1990s, scientists began to discover that we can indeed grow new neurons. First animal studies, and later research on humans proved that we can grow new brain cells as we age.

The human brain is an amazing organ. It's the central control system for your entire body. Without a well-functioning brain, you wouldn't breathe, digest your food or move your limbs. It can compensate for injuries, re-route nerve pathways when necessary and even re-purpose unused areas.

Genetics play a large role in long-term brain health. If you have a grandmother or grandfather, father, mother or sister or brother with Alzheimer's disease (AD) or dementia, your risk of developing the disease is two to three times greater than that of someone with no family connections to the disease. If you have more than one family member with the disease, your risk further increases and so your concern should increase, leading you to take the preventive measures described in Chapters 4 and 5.

If I were facing life with a grandfather with AD and perhaps a parent who was beginning to decline, I'll tell you that I'd do everything possible to improve my odds of keeping my memory intact. I'd be out there learning languages, doing crossword puzzles and sudoku, taking tango lessons, eating the best possible diet and taking the right supplements.

Putting early and intense effort into increasing your brain power will improve your odds and give you better chances of slowing down cognitive decline or even eliminating it altogether.

THOSE "MOMENTS"

How alarmed should you be when those "moments" occur?

Forgetting where you left your car keys, groping for a word or missing an important appointment does not mean your memory is failing.

It happens to the best of us, at any stage of life.

These kinds of memory lapses can be caused by stress, lack of sleep or simply having too much on your plate.

It's sometimes called "tip of the tongue phenomena." It happens to everybody. Don't fret about it.

I like to think of the memory like the hard drive on a computer. So, over the years, we fill our minds with information, experiences, memories, faces, numbers and all sorts of "stuff."

There is a hierarchy of information that goes into that hard drive.

No one expects you to remember what you ate for lunch last Wednesday or what you wore to a party six months ago or your address ten years ago. These things are simply not important enough for long-term storage in your memory. Even the more important minutiae of daily life, like the exact time of your next dentist's appointment or your driver's license number, probably aren't worth taking up "hard drive space" when you can keep an appointment book and other written records.

Short-term memories are probably stored electrically. Unless it's something that has some bearing on your life, you won't remember it long term because it is not necessary. They just shoot through your brain like an electrical impulse and are gone. Of course, if some urgent circumstance occurs in which you need to remember where you ate lunch a week ago, because there was a hepatitis outbreak at a restaurant you frequent, you could probably recall the information; but you probably couldn't recover it without the help of your PDA if the lunch in question was six months ago.

Memories that you use on a regular basis have a chemical base. Your brain actually lays down a protein that roots those memories in your brain tissue. For example, you probably have some strong childhood recollections, perhaps of family holiday gatherings or visits or your mother's face or the smell of your grandmother's pies in the oven. Long-term memories can be quite complex. For example, you may hear a familiar song from the 1960s and immediately you are transported back to an event that you can see and hear in your mind which may also include intense emotion. Just hearing a few notes from a song can stimulate the visual and auditory cortex as well as the emotional centers of your brain. Because those memories are an important part of who you are, they are chemically stored in your brain.

As you age, it can sometimes become harder to remember some of these little things.

That's perfectly normal and should not be cause for worry.

All memory lapses are not Alzheimer's disease or dementia.

It's a different story if your neurons start misfiring and you can no longer tell a friend the details of the latest book you're reading or you can't recall your way home from the grocery store or remember that you left your car keys in the freezer.

There is another type of cognitive dysfunction related to depression called pseudo-dementia. Common in older people, pseudo-dementia manifests as a failing memory which is actually caused by the underlying depression. Fortunately, for these patients, treating the depression usually takes care of the memory problem.

Sometimes patients will come to my office alone, complaining they are worried about increasingly frequent memory lapses. It's a good sign for me if the patient is alone. That means he recognizes he may have a problem. Most patients with Alzheimer's or other forms of dementia frequently don't recognize their own problem.

I usually ask these patients two questions:
- Is your family complaining about your memory lapses?
- Are your memory lapses affecting your ability to perform your job efficiently?

If the answer to both of these questions is "No," I breathe a sigh of relief. If family is not complaining of memory loss and job performance is acceptable, it is very likely the memory lapses are due to stress, poor sleep quality or simple mental overload rather than due to dementia. Making small adjustments in these three areas will usually resolve the problem.

It's a different story when a family member accompanies a patient to my office and complains about the patient's memory loss. The patient who is suffering from early or middle stages of AD or dementia is usually not aware of the extent and severity of the problem. This loss of self-awareness is a sign that dementia has set in and is a serious problem. It is very sad because the patient may be sitting there with family, friendly and smiling, seemingly without a care in the world when he/she is quite literally losing his/her mind. That's perhaps the only good part about the disease: the victims really don't suffer much because they are usually not cognizant enough to realize what they have lost and what they will lose as times goes on.

The torture has just begun for the family who must care for the patient as the disease takes its toll until the patient is little more than an infant, with needs that must be addressed 24 hours a day, seven days a week.

THE LEARNING CURVE

Lifelong learning is probably the single most powerful way to keep your brain function intact.

That's because when you learn something, anything from how to tie your shoes to a foreign language, your brain cells communicate that information and remember it. The more pieces of information you learn and remember, the more connective pathways there are between your brain cells.

A case in point: The Talmud, the Jewish sacred book of laws, ethics, customs and history, is 2,711 pages long. Many orthodox Jews study the book on a daily basis, memorize the entire book and spend their lives arguing the complex points of law and theology the Talmud contains. I have seen 90-year-old men, Talmudic scholars, who are very conversant in the complexities of the text. They have intensively challenged their brains for their entire lives and their brains have paid them back by remaining fully functional. That's because when AD or other dementia causes some of the neural pathways to malfunction, extensive mental challenges and learning have forged multiple pathways for the thought and memory patterns to travel, and the brain can automatically re-route the information by one of the other multiple networks, and memory isn't impaired.

AD doesn't mean the person is no longer intelligent; the intellect remains intact, but the ability to retrieve the information is impaired.

Most of us don't challenge our brains enough, early in life or later. If you are doing the same rote (memorized) tasks every day, your brain isn't being stimulated.

If you don't use it, you'll lose it.

One of the most exciting long-term studies on lifelong brain health and risks of AD was conducted by David Snowdon, Ph.D., on a group of Roman Catholic nuns. Dr. Snowdon began his research in 1986 with nearly 700 members of the teaching Sisters of Notre Dame, ages 75 to 106. His research continues to this day. I'll be citing many of the groundbreaking findings of the Nun Study throughout this book.

Dr. Snowdon's most significant studies about the importance of early education and lifelong learning showed that educational achievement is vital to continued brain health throughout life and that some active, educated women whose brains actually showed the pathological changes of advanced Alzheimer's disease were actually able to function with normal memories until their deaths, often at a very advanced age.

In a more recent study published in the June 2007 edition of the journal *Neurology*, researchers from Chicago followed more than 700 elderly (average age 80) people yearly for five years. By the end of the study, 90 had developed Alzheimer's disease. It was found that frequent participation in activities involving mental activity was associated with a 50% reduced incidence of Alzheimer's disease. A mentally inactive person in old age was 2.6 times more likely to develop Alzheimer's than those who were mentally active. Brain autopsies were performed in over 100 subjects who died during the study which failed to show a correlation between level of mental activity and pathologic changes in the brain. Dr. Robert Wilson, the lead author of the study, indicated that mental inactivity is "truly a risk factor for Alzheimer's and not simply an early consequence of the disease."

THE DOWN SIDE

While our brains have these impressive restorative abilities, and while there is a great deal we can do to preserve brain function and memory, time takes its toll. Eventually, we begin to lose some mental function.

The older you get, the less productive and the less efficient your brain function becomes. Statistics show that 50 percent of all people over 85 have Alzheimer's disease (AD), dementia or cognitive impairment in some form. While the percentages of those with AD are much lower at younger ages, it is clear that the aging process itself does certainly lead to some degree of memory impairment and loss of neural connections.

Physical impairments are also a part of aging. The ability to walk, see and hear becomes impaired as the cells age and are not replaced. That's just a reality. People with physical impairments may not have AD or other cognitive disorders, but they may become fearful, afraid of falling, driving at night, maybe even going outside. That affects their entire lives, too.

You may have noticed I said that the memory loss can take the form of Alzheimer's disease, dementia and cognitive impairment. I'll go into more details and specifics of what this means in the coming chapters.

I'll be straightforward with you. There is usually a very grim prognosis for those with Alzheimer's and dementia.

Dr. Snowdon suggests that diagnosis is delayed in many patients with AD and dementia because of what he calls "ageism—the prejudice that failing capacities are normal for the elderly." By making those assumptions, Dr. Snowdon theorizes, treatment frequently begins only after symptoms have been present for several years.

We do not have effective treatments for this disease. While there are some prescription drugs that may slow the progress of the disease somewhat, they are usually not very effective.

Symptoms usually do not appear until the disease has progressed beyond the abilities of medical science to effectively treat it.

AD takes a terrible toll on families. They go to sleep at night praying the nightmare of a loved one fading away will be gone, and they awaken in the morning to find it is all still there and each day is a little worse than the day before.

And it is always fatal, but the average time between diagnosis and death may be as long as 12 years or more.

Beyond loving them and caring for them as long as you can, there's not much of anything you can do for your aging parent or grandparent who is slipping into this abyss.

However, there is a great deal you can do for yourself and your family to delay the onset of these diseases, to slow the progress and perhaps to even prevent them altogether, if you start early enough.

MEMORY LOSS MAY MEAN SIMPLY GROWING OLDER

The memory loss that frequently accompanies aging has a name, age-related cognitive decline (ARCD). It's not considered a disease because many authorities think this loss of memory is a normal part of aging. People with ARCD experience gradual deterioration in memory and learning, attention and concentration, thinking, use of language and other mental functions.

For most people, as they age, cognitive performance remains reasonably stable over time, with only slight declines in short-term memory and reaction time.

Some older people have more memory and cognitive difficulties than those of normal aging, but their symptoms are not so severe as to justify a diagnosis of Alzheimer's disease. Some of these people go on to develop AD while many do not. This middle category is often called "mild cognitive impairment (MCI)" or "mild neurocognitive disorder." Although as a rule stress does not lead to long-term cognitive impairment, a recent study published in the journal *Neurology* suggested that chronic psychological distress was associated with increased incidence of MCI.

Sudden memory loss or other symptoms of cognitive decline are not a part of normal aging. More rapid mental deterioration may be an indicator of AD or another type of dementia.

IN CONCLUSION

Aging does not mean the inevitable loss of memory.

True, it happens to some of us, to many of us. But you can take steps at any time in your life to preserve your memory.

If you're concerned that you are starting to be forgetful, whatever your age, become proactive, change your life and keep your mind.

References:

Glei DA, Landau DA et al. Participating in social activities helps preserve cognitive function: an analysis of a longitudinal, population-based study of the elderly. International Journal of Epidemiology 2005; 34(4):864-871.

Yu F, Kolanowski AM et al. Improving cognition and function through exercise intervention in Alzheimer's disease. Journal of Nursing Scholarship 2006;38(4):358-65.

Pinilla FG. The impact of diet and exercise on brain plasticity and disease. Nutrition and Health 2006;18(3):277-84.

Cameron HA, Woolley CS et al. Differentiation of newly born neurons and glia in the dentate gyrus of the adult rat. Neuroscience 1993 Sep;56(2):337-44.

Eriksson PS, Perfilieva E et al. Neurogenesis in the adult human hippocampus. Nature Medicine 1998 Nov;4(11):1313-7.

Mortimer JA, Snowdon DA et al. Head circumference and risk of dementia: findings from the Nun Study. Journal of Clinical and Experimental Neuropsychology 2003 Aug;25(5):671-9.

Snowdon DA. Healthy aging and dementia: findings from the Nun Study. Annals of Internal Medicine 2003 Sep 2;139(5 Pt 2):450-4.

Craik FIM, Salthouse TA. Handbook of Aging and Cognition. Hillsdale, NJ (Erlbaum, 1992).

Smith GE, Petersen RC, Parisi JE et al. Definition, course, and outcome of mild cognitive impairment. Aging, Neuropsychology and Cognition 1996;3:141-7.

Rubin EH, Storandt M, Miller JP et al. A prospective study of cognitive function and onset of dementia in cognitively healthy elders. Archives of Neurology 1998;55(3):395–401.

Wilson RS, Schneider JA et al. Chronic distress and incidence of mild cognitive impairment. Neurology 2007;68:2085-2092.

Wilson RS, Scherr PA et al. The relation of cognitive activity to risk of developing Alzheimer's disease. Neurology 2007, [Epub ahead of print].

For more on the Nun Study:

Snowdon, David, Aging with Grace (Bantam, 2001).

Anatomy of Brain, Mind and Memory

We all want to minimize our risks for cognitive dysfunction. In order to do so, it's important to have at least an elementary understanding of how your brain and memory work.

I know. I can hear you groaning. I promise to make the learning process as painless as possible and as simple as I can. If you really can't bear it, skip this chapter, but I think if you stick with me, you'll be glad you did. Consider it a form of mental exercise. It's good for you and tastes better than cod liver oil.

BRAIN FUNCTION 101

The human brain is a masterpiece of engineering—computer engineering, if you will.

Scientists have only touched the tip of the iceberg in understanding the complexity of this organ comprised of 100 billion neurons or single nerve cells that send and receive messages.

These messages travel as minute electrical impulses across an intricate network of dendrites, root-like extensions of the nerve cells that reach out to one another. One single neuron can have hundreds of thousands of dendrites, comprising a truly awe-inspiring network that is far more complex than even the most complex computers known today.

The information or thoughts jump across the miniscule spaces between dendrites called synapses with the help of specialized chemical messengers called neurotransmitters, racing around the neuronal network at lightning speed.

The more the neural pathways are used, the stronger they become and the more dendrites a single neuron might have.

Think of your dendrites as highways for thoughts and memories. The more you have, the more alternative routes there are to your destination. What this means is that if sometime in the future, you develop a disease that affects your brain, the effect will be diminished because of your expanded brain transit system.

The brain is the body's command central. It controls autonomic or unconscious functions, among them breathing, heartbeat and digestion. It's also responsible for conscious functions like muscle movement, vision and hunger.

What's even more exciting about the human brain is that this little three-pound organ is responsible for what makes each of us a unique individual: thoughts, feelings, emotions, talents, memories and the ability to learn, remember and process information.

The brain has these main parts:

Brain stem: Sitting at the base of the skull atop the spinal cord, the brain stem, also known as the reptilian brain, controls basic biological functions like breathing, blood pressure and heartbeat. It's also the relay point for messages from the brain to the rest of the body and vice versa. That's why an injury at this point often leads to paralysis.

Cerebellum: Just above the brain stem, the cerebellum controls muscle movement, including coordination, muscle tone and equilibrium. As we age, the cerebellum has a memory function that helps us recall certain types of movement. For example, you may have struggled to learn the balance and coordination necessary to learn to ice skate. Once your body figured out how to remain upright and glide across the ice, the memory of those brain signals became embedded in your brain. Even if you didn't skate for 30 years, with a little initial wobbliness, your brain would quickly remember the skills necessary to stay upright, even if you're no Sasha Cohen.

Cerebrum: Also called the mammalian brain because it's what differentiates mammals from other life forms, the cerebrum is divided into right and left hemispheres. The left side of the cerebrum controls language and mathematical abilities and the right side controls abstract thinking, emotions, the aesthetic senses and visualization.

Each hemisphere is divided into four lobes, each with a particular function and all of them with many shared functions.

- The **frontal lobes** are the seat of learning and speaking. They govern problem solving, deliberation, judgment and the ability to control our impulses so we (generally) behave in a socially acceptable manner.
- The **temporal lobes** (located near the temples) are where hearing, the ability to understand language and short-term memories reside.
- The **parietal lobes** are associated with perception and sensation. They forge the links between new information and stored memories and relay information between the various lobes of the cerebrum.
- The **occipital lobes** near the base of the brain govern vision and visual memories.

Limbic system: This region surrounds the top of the brain stem and generally governs emotions, ranging from love and sexual behavior, compassion and pleasure to fear, anger and aggression. It is composed of four sections:

- The **hippocampus** is the control center for learning and short-term and long-term memories. The hippocampus governs our ability to learn new skills. It acts like a relay station, processing new memories and routing them to other parts of the brain. The hippocampus is often the first part of the brain affected in people with Alzheimer's disease, which explains why people with AD often become forgetful about recent events and can become lost in familiar places. We'll be talking about the hippocampus a great deal in Chapter 4.
- The **amygdala** is the emotional response center. Among many functions, the amygdala helps determine how deeply ingrained the chemical response to a memory becomes and how long the memory is retained. The depth of memory retention is often dependent on the strength of the emotions attached to the event, so the amygdala is the gatekeeper of emotional memories. That explains why we may have very strong memories of an emotionally charged event like falling out of a tree and breaking an arm, but little memory of the toys we played with as children.
- The **thalamus** is the body's pain center and also governs sensory impulses, taste and touch, but not smell.
- The **hypothalamus** regulates the involuntary nervous system and the endocrine gland system, body temperature, hunger, sugar and fat metabolism and sexual behavior.

MEMORY FUNCTION 101

If the human brain is the command center of the body, the memory is the retrieval system for everything we know, say, see, smell, taste, touch and feel. The human memory and the way we retrieve information is immensely complex.

While we know memory is complex, modern science is still learning where it physically resides and how it functions.

Dr. Eric Kandel, who won the Nobel Prize in 2000 for his research on memory, explains, "(Memory) It's extraordinary. It's the glue that ties the fabric of our mental life together. I can sit here and do mental time travel. I can think about my childhood in Vienna, I can think about my first date, I can think about getting married, I can think of going to medical school ... with an enormous facility, I can move back and forth in my mind between different events that occurred because of the powers of my memory to do this."

Memories are not stored like snapshots in your brain. There are many impressions—as sights, sounds and other information—stored in various parts of the brain. They are also stored in the parts of the brain that initially processed the information. It makes the analogy of a giant hard drive even

ILLUSTRATION OF THE BRAIN

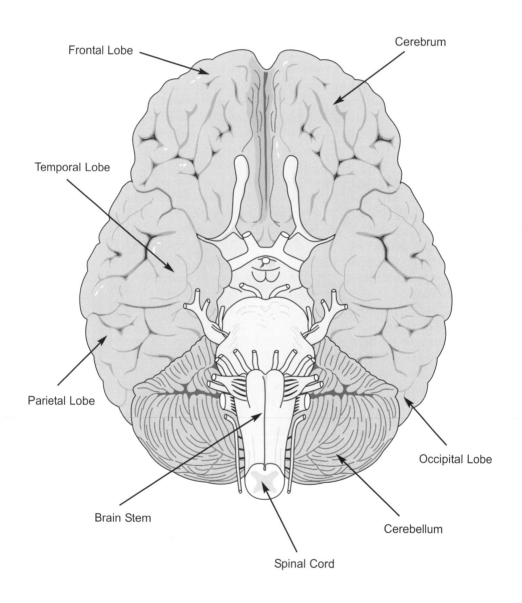

Frontal Lobe

Cerebrum

Temporal Lobe

Parietal Lobe

Occipital Lobe

Brain Stem

Cerebellum

Spinal Cord

more apt, since the data is scattered around everywhere. If you've ever tried to uninstall a program from your computer, you know that programs are not blocks of data, they're more like spider webs that spread out all over the place.

So if, over time, you forgot who was at your fifth birthday party because it isn't terribly important, you may still retain the memory of the pony rides you and your friends took to celebrate or the taste of the cake or the fall you took and skinned your knee.

Memories are essential to our lives. They define us, and they are who each of us happens to be. When we recall a memory, we don't just open a file drawer in the memory banks and pull out the file. We cast around and pull out the memories from a wide variety of places.

The Brain Wide Web, or BWW if you will, that accesses these memories is made up of nerve cells connecting at the junctions between the dendrites called synapses. The more connections there are, the stronger the memory.

Emotions attached to memories make them stronger.

From the above section on brain function, you know that certain areas of the brain are responsible for short-term memories. The hippocampus, the amygdala, the cerebellum and the temporal lobes of the cerebrum all have specialized roles in memory retention.

We know that there is no single part of the brain where we can pinpoint the location of your memory.

Here are a few more things we know:
- Thoughts race between neurons, with the help of neurotransmitters.
- These thoughts actually become physical pathways that can connect several parts of the brain. For example, if you've just learned something like a new word or you've met someone new or you're trying to identify a piece of music, the neuron network may connect several different parts of your brain to help you visualize that new face or recall an audio memory.
- Some scientists say we have millions of billions of these pathways in our brains.
- These neuronal pathways hang on to those memories in some way that is not entirely understood by science. Some scientists theorize the memory pathway actually alters the RNA pathways of the neurons, possibly through some type of protein alteration.
- New memories can create new dendrites and new network connections.
- The more you use a particular pathway, the more deeply it is laid down.

- Conversely, new learning and new experiences forge new pathways. For example, if you always put on your left sock first, your brain will have a deep imprint based on years of daily experience that this is the way to do it. If you focus on putting on your right sock first, after a couple of weeks, your brain will recognize this as an acceptable way to accomplish the task and it won't feel so "wrong" anymore.
- Certain proteins are responsible for converting short-term memories to long-term memories and without them, these long-term memories cannot be formed.
- When a network fails because of Alzheimer's disease or other forms of dementia, the more networks that exist, the more alternative pathways there are that can carry the same memories and the same information, so the less impairment there will be.

You may remember that I mentioned in Chapter 1 my admiration for Dr. David Snowdon's work with the Nun Study. In working with this large group of women, most of whom were teachers and can be presumed to be intelligent and highly educated, he found that some had clearly forged alternative neuronal pathways that kept their memories intact.

Alzheimer's disease can be extremely difficult to diagnose with absolute certainty. It can only be definitively diagnosed through an autopsy or brain biopsy by physically observing the microscopic presence of characteristic lesions, tangles and plaques in the brain tissue.

That's exactly what Snowdon did. All the women who participated in his study agreed to annual cognitive function tests and to donate their brains to research after their deaths.

He had some surprising findings:

"Most of the brains neatly fit our expectations, with little or no evidence of disease in a tack-sharp sister and abundant damage seen in a sister who had dementia," he wrote in Aging with Grace. But sometimes (we find) little evidence of Alzheimer's in a sister who had the classic symptoms of the disease. And sometimes the brains of sisters who appeared mentally intact when alive showed extensive evidence of Alzheimer's."

If you've used your brain extensively throughout your life, in your early years, middle years and old age, you are much more likely to remain mentally intact.

An interesting 2002 study at Massachusetts Institute of Technology actually mapped the pathways through which at least some memories were stored. A group of healthy young people underwent MRI screening. Researchers tested their memories for a list of words and then gave subjects a pop quiz 20 minutes later. The MRIs were able to identify the ideas that were going to be shunted to long-term memory and those that would be deleted.

It's still very early in the game with this concept, but it is possible that doctors in the future will be able to map deviations from baseline memory pathways to diagnose early memory problems.

THE INCREDIBLE STRETCHABLE BRAIN

Neuroplasticity is the term for the kinds of changes that take place in the human brain as we age and demonstrate our ability to absorb new information and make the physical and mental changes that this new information might dictate.

Neuroplasticity doesn't mean your brain is plastic. It means it is moldable, changeable. It compensates for obstacles. It adapts. It adjusts.

It also means that your brain can re-route pathways to access information and memories if some of the pathways are damaged by an injury, stroke, Alzheimer's or other forms of dementia.

One fascinating German study showed that the right sides of the cerebrums of violin players were larger than normal because of the additional stimulation and growth of neuronal pathways caused by playing the strings with their left hands. While that might be expected in children, the German researchers found that adults could also expand the size of their already-fully-developed right brains by learning to play the violin.

The Society for Neuroscience has some even more astounding examples of neuroplasticity in blind people, young and old, whose brains actually adapted to use some of the idle visual centers in their brains to increase their ability to read Braille.

NEUROTRANSMITTERS

I'd like to add just a few words about the importance of neurotransmitters, those brain chemicals that carry the electrical impulses between neurons.

There are presumably dozens of them, but the most important to memory and learning (that scientists have discovered thus far) are:

Acetylcholine: Concentrated in the hippocampus and frontal lobes, it plays a key role in learning and memory. Studies show that people with Alzheimer's are almost always deficient in acetylcholine.

Norepinephrine: Also known as noradrenaline, this neurotransmitter is part of the process of forming long-term memories, especially those that are related to painful, frightening or otherwise emotion-laden events. It's the body's norepinephrine response that helps you remember the painful consequences of putting your hand on a hot stove. While this hormone helps keep you alert, an excess can lead to chronic stress, with lots of negative effects.

GABA: Short for gamma aminobutyric acid, this calming neurotransmitter slows down rapidly firing neurons that can result in your brain becoming overstimulated and resulting in anxiety. Ideally, we want a good balance between GABA and the stimulating neurotransmitters glutamate and dopamine, which both have effects on memory.

Serotonin: Also known as the "feel-good" brain chemical, serotonin naturally lifts your mood, counteracting depressive tendencies. Since we know that depression is a risk factor for cognitive dysfunction, it's important to keep serotonin at an optimal level.

IN CONCLUSION

You don't have to be an auto mechanic to own a car and drive it quite successfully. Nor do you have to be a computer geek to use a computer in your everyday tasks and get along very well.

And, of course, you don't have to know all the intricacies of the brain to understand what you need to do to keep yours healthy.

This has been the barest of bare bones explanation of how your brain and memory work. I've simply given you the basics here so you'll have a resource for various terms related to brain function and a general idea of what I'm talking about in the next chapter, which explains what happens when things go wrong in your brain, and in the following chapter, which helps you understand how to keep things from going wrong in the first place.

References:

Lee CT, Ma YL. Serum- and glucocorticoid-inducible kinase1 enhances contextual fear memory formation through down-regulation of the expression of Hes5. Journal of Neurochemistry 2007 Jan 15;100(6):1531-42.

Qian Z, Gilbert ME et al. Tissue plasminogen activator is induced as an immediate-early gene during seizure, kindling and long-term potentiation. Nature 1993 Feb 4;361(6411):453-7.

Pang PT, Teng HK et al. Cleavage of proBDNF by tPA/plasmin is essential for long-term hippocampal plasticity. Science 2004 Oct 15;306(5695):487-91.

Davachi L, Mitchell JP et al. Multiple routes to memory: distinct medial temporal lobe processes build item and source memories. Proceedings of the National Academy of Sciences of the USA 2003 Feb 18;100(4)2157-62.

Shahin A, Bosnyak DJ et al. Enhancement of neuroplastic P2 and N1c auditory evoked potentials in musicians. Journal of Neuroscience 2003 Jul 2;23(13):5545-52.

Gizewski ER, Gasser T et al. Cross-model plasticity for sensory and motor activation patterns in blind subjects. NeuroImage 2003 Jul;19(3):968-75.

Theoret H, Merabet L et al. Behavioral and neuroplastic changes in the blind: evidence for functionally cross-modal interactions. Journal de Physiologie (Paris) 2004 Jan-Jun;98(1-3):221-33.

Thogi H, Abe T et al. Remarkable reduction in acetylcholine concentration in the cerebrospinal fluid from patients with Alzheimer type dementia. Neuroscience Letters 1994 Aug 15;177(1-2):139-42.

When Things Go Wrong: Alzheimer's and Other Forms of Dementia

It is truly tragic when the complex computer that is the human brain begins to malfunction, the messages are lost or garbled and brain cells die.

AN OVERVIEW

Dementia is a general term for loss of memory and other mental abilities severe enough to interfere with daily life.

Alzheimer's disease (AD) is the most common form of dementia, accounting for 50 to 70 percent of the cases and believed to affect 20 to 25 million people worldwide and four to five million Americans. Experts project a fourfold increase in the number of cases worldwide by 2050. But AD is only one of a dozen conditions that results in the gradual destruction of brain cells and leads to progressive decline in mental function.

The terms Alzheimer's disease and dementia are sometimes used interchangeably, but they are not the same thing. Some forms of dementia have very different characteristics.

AD is characterized by physical changes in the brain that accompany a unique type of protein called beta amyloid plaques and neurofibrillary fibers that cause characteristic tangles in the brain tissue. No one really knows if the plaques and tangles actually cause AD or if they develop after the fact.

AD destroys a person's memory and ability to learn, reason, make judgments, communicate and carry out daily tasks.

It affects the parts of the brain that control memory and reasoning skills, but as the disease progresses, cells die in other parts of the brain.

As the patient declines further, there may be changes in personality and behavior. Anxiety, suspiciousness, aggressiveness or agitation, as well as delusions or hallucinations are among the many personality changes that can take place with AD.

Eventually, the victim will require complete care.

Finally, the person with AD will be bedridden. Pneumonia and infections from bedsores are the most common causes of death in people with Alzheimer's, not the disease itself. The time from diagnosis to death can range from three to 20 years, with a continuous decline throughout that time period.

No one really knows what causes Alzheimer's, although there are many risk factors which I'll explore in detail in the next two chapters.

There is no doubt about it: Alzheimer's and dementia are grim topics. If you have a family member or loved one with the disease, it's important to know what is happening and what will happen. It's also important to know the mechanics of the disease so you can do whatever is necessary to prevent, delay or slow the progression of dementia in yourself and your family and friends.

No one knows what causes Alzheimer's disease, and there is no really effective treatment for it.

It's almost impossible to say anything positive about Alzheimer's disease. I guess the only hopeful thing I can say is that the burden of the disease falls on the family and caregivers. The victims of progressing AD are almost always blissfully unaware of their condition. Frequently they smile and are cheerful. Sorry folks, that's about as good as I can do to be positive about this devastating condition.

As I promised in the last chapter, I'll make this as painless as possible.

WHAT CAUSES ALZHEIMER'S

If we knew precisely what causes AD, we'd be well on our way to finding a cure. There's a great deal of Catch-22 in the current research. Beta amyloid plaques are characteristic of AD, and scientists have recently learned that a particular type of protein called tau protein starts the process of tangling neurofibers, beginning the cascade of events that leads to AD. But the plaques and tangles can only definitively be diagnosed by a brain biopsy or an autopsy. That's not very helpful if we're looking for tools to bring about an early diagnosis.

There are some promising new diagnostic testing methods, but they're not yet ready for prime time.

We do know that beta amyloid plaques and tau protein-based neurofibrillary tangles cause the characteristic plaques and tangles that are present in nearly everyone with AD; but as I said before, these plaques are visible only on a microscopic level. Sometimes there is a reason to do a biopsy on a person with suspected AD, but this is not a common diagnostic tool.

These plaques and tangles, which usually begin in the hippocampus where short-term memory resides, reduce the number of dendrites per neuron, impairing communication between nerve cells. They eventually cause brain cells to die.

Age and genetic background are the two most widely recognized risk factors for AD. Despite a recent wave of early-onset dementia, the disease is thankfully rare in people under 60. After the age of 65, the risk of AD doubles every five years. About half of all Americans over 85 have AD.

Genetic predisposition to AD is well documented.

Scientists have identified a "risk gene" called apoliprotein E-e4 or APOE-e4 that dramatically increases the risk of AD. Everyone has the APOE gene, but if you have inherited the APOE-e4, your risk of AD is increased. If you have inherited it from both parents, your risk is even higher. People with APOE-e4 are also at risk of developing early onset AD. Yet the presence of APOE-e4 does not guarantee that you'll get AD.

There are also genes called deterministic genes that directly cause a disease, guaranteeing that anyone who inherits them will develop the disorder. Scientists have found these rare types of genes that directly cause Alzheimer's in only a few hundred extended families around the world.

When Alzheimer's disease is caused by deterministic genes, it is called "familial Alzheimer's disease," and many family members in multiple generations are affected. The only good news about familial Alzheimer's is that it accounts for fewer than five percent of cases.

While it is technically possible (although expensive) to be genetically tested for both the high risk APOE-e4 gene and the rare genes that directly cause Alzheimer's, health professionals usually do not recommend routine genetic testing for AD. Testing for APOE-e4 is sometimes included as a part of research studies.

Scientists have also discovered a relationship between blood levels of homocysteine, an amino acid produced as part of the normal human metabolism, and cognitive decline. High homocysteine levels have been thought to literally poison the nervous system as well as the cardiovascular system, making this a potential double whammy for Alzheimer's and dementia.

Environmental factors may also be a factor in the development of AD and dementia. For example, one animal study suggests that excess copper can cause elevated levels of homocysteine. Other studies suggest that pesticides may increase the risk of Parkinson's disease and the dementia that frequently occurs in the end stages of the disease. Other research links exceptionally high levels of iron in the brain to AD.

SYMPTOMS

Families of people with Alzheimer's most often miss the early symptoms of AD because they seem unimportant. Most frequently, the early stages are characterized by mild forgetfulness or disorientation.

In the early stage of AD, there may be trouble remembering recent events, activities, or the names of familiar people or things. Solving simple math problems or balancing a checkbook may become very difficult. These shortcomings may be a nuisance, but they are usually not serious enough to cause alarm.

That is why AD often is not diagnosed until it has reached the moderate to severe stage, when pharmaceuticals designed to slow the progress of the disease are usually only minimally effective.

If you or someone you love begins to suffer any of these symptoms, it's best to check them out early rather than to discount them as normal signs of aging. The earlier treatment and preventive measures begin, the more likely it is that you can help slow the progress of the disease.

> *Symptoms of Alzheimer's and other forms of dementia frequently go unnoticed until the disease has reached a stage where there are no real effective treatment options.*

IDENTIFYING THE STAGES OF AD

I'm sharing these with you in order to give you some mileposts if you are dealing with a loved one with impaired cognitive function—or if you suspect it in yourself.

There are three stages of Alzheimer's: mild, moderate and severe. These often hold true for other types of dementia.

Mild
• Repetition of stories.
• Lack of initiative to start projects.
• Giving up the checkbook.
• Some word finding difficulty.
• Some change in personality.

Moderate AD (This is the stage where relatives most often bring the patient to me)
• Loses recent memory.
• Loses judgment about money.
• Has difficulty with new learning and making new memories.
• Has trouble finding words—may substitute or make up words that sound like or mean something like the forgotten word.
• May stop talking to avoid making mistakes.
• Has shorter attention span and less motivation to stay with an activity.

- Easily loses way going to familiar places.
- Resists change or new things.
- Has trouble organizing and thinking logically.
- Asks repetitive questions.
- Withdraws, loses interest, is irritable, not as sensitive to others' feelings, uncharacteristically angry when frustrated or tired.
- Won't make decisions. For example, when asked what he wants to eat, says "I'll have what she is having."
- Takes longer to do routine chores and becomes upset if rushed or if something unexpected happens.
- Forgets to pay, pays too much, or forgets how to pay; may hand the checkout person a wallet instead of the correct amount of money.
- Loses or misplaces things by hiding them in odd places or forgets where things go, such as putting clothes in the dishwasher.
- Constantly checks, searches or hoards things of no value.
- Gives up driving.
- Forgets to eat, eats only one kind of food, or eats constantly.
- Changes in behavior, concern for appearance, hygiene, and sleep become more noticeable.
- Poor judgment creates safety issues when left alone; may wander and risk exposure, poisoning, falls, self-neglect or exploitation.
- Has trouble recognizing familiar people and her own objects; may take things that belong to others.
- Continuously repeats stories, favorite words, statements, or motions like tearing tissues.
- Has restless, repetitive movements in late afternoon or evening (known as sundowner effect) such as pacing, trying doorknobs, fingering draperies.
- Cannot organize thoughts or follow logical explanations.
- Has trouble following written notes or completing tasks.
- Makes up stories to fill in gaps in memory. For example might say, "Mama will come for me when she gets off work."
- May be able to read but cannot formulate the correct response to a written request.
- May accuse, threaten, curse, fidget or behave inappropriately, such as kicking, hitting, biting, screaming or grabbing.
- Neglects personal hygiene.
- May become sloppy or forget manners.
- May see, hear, smell, or taste things that are not there.
- May accuse spouse of an affair or family members of stealing.
- Naps frequently or awakens at night believing it is time to go

to work.
- Has more difficulty positioning the body to use the toilet or sit in a chair.
- Needs help finding the toilet, using the shower, remembering to drink and dressing for the weather or occasion.
- Exhibits inappropriate sexual behavior, such as mistaking another individual for a spouse. Forgets what should be private behavior and may disrobe or masturbate in public.

Severe AD
- Doesn't recognize close family.
- Speaks in gibberish, is mute or is difficult to understand.
- May refuse to eat, choke or forget to swallow.
- May repetitively cry out, pat or touch things.
- Loses control of bowel and bladder.
- Loses weight and skin becomes thin and tears easily.
- May look uncomfortable or cry out when transferred or touched.
- Forgets how to walk or is too unsteady or weak to stand alone.
- May have seizures, frequent infections, falls.
- May groan, scream or mumble loudly.
- Sleeps more.
- Needs total assistance for all activities of daily living.

When a patient reaches the severe stage, placement in a skilled nursing facility is almost inevitable. Few families are equipped emotionally, physically or financially to provide the constant care that is required.

EARLY ONSET ALZHEIMER'S

In recent years, the medical community has increasingly begun to recognize early onset AD, which usually means the symptoms begin before the age of 65. Symptoms have been known to develop in people as young as 30, but that is exceedingly rare. Most cases of early onset Alzheimer's begin in the 40s or 50s.

Early onset Alzheimer's has been linked to the genetic predisposition to the disease caused by the APOE-e4 gene. It is estimated that six to eight percent of people with AD, or about 300,000 people in the U.S., have the early onset form.

While Alzheimer's can have a devastating effect at any age, early onset Alzheimer's is particularly devastating. We don't expect younger people to have Alzheimer's. These are typically people who still have work and family responsibilities. The effects of the disease can cause them to be fired from jobs or severely impair their relationships.

In addition to age, there are other differences between early onset and late-onset Alzheimer's disease (otherwise known as senile dementia of the

Alzheimer's type, or SDAT), including:
- Younger people who develop Alzheimer's disease tend to have more of the microscopic changes found in the brain than that of older people with Alzheimer's disease. These changes include tangles and plaques that damage the healthy brain cells that surround them, causing the brain to waste away and shrink. Some experts believe that younger brains need to suffer more damage before the person starts to show symptoms, making early diagnosis more difficult.
- A substantial majority of early onset Alzheimer's disease appears to be linked with a genetic defect on chromosome 14, to which late-onset Alzheimer's is not linked.
- A condition called myoclonus—muscle twitching and spasm—is more commonly seen in early onset AD than in late-onset AD.
- Some research suggests that people with early onset AD decline at a faster rate than do those with late-onset AD.

TYPES OF NON-ALZHEIMER'S DEMENTIA

As I said before, not all dementia is Alzheimer's. Here are some of the more common non-Alzheimer's types of dementia:

Vascular dementia (sometimes known as multi-infarct dementia), caused by a series of small strokes, is the second most common type of dementia. People with vascular dementia may exhibit some memory loss, but the symptoms more often include difficulty with the thinking process, walking, bladder control and vision. It is possible to have vascular dementia and Alzheimer's at the same time, affecting different parts of the brain depending on where the stroke left its mark.

Dementia with Lewy bodies is another common form of dementia, particularly among older people. These Lewy bodies are distinctive protein deposits on the nerve cells, but their cause is unknown. It is rarely the cause of early onset dementia and the accompanying deterioration is usually more rapid. The symptoms are similar to AD, with the additions of rapid fluctuations in lucidity and delirium, delusions, hallucinations, rigid limbs and a characteristic lurching forward when starting to walk and stumbling when coming to a stop. People with Lewy body dementia often hallucinate that children, adults, animals and grotesque characters in costumes have intruded their homes. One characteristic hallucination is that these characters are wearing elaborate hats and/or that they have lattice or grid patterns over their faces.

Pick's disease more often affects younger people under the age of 65. It is characterized by personality changes that may be apparent before memory lapses occur. Those personality changes often include inappropriate behavior in public, speaking loudly or rudely or impatiently or becoming withdrawn and depressed. Patients with Pick's often compulsively place things in their mouths. Because Pick's disease can occur in people as young as 20, it is often diagnosed as a psychiatric disorder. It is most often found in people between the ages of 50 and 60.

Frontotemporal dementia. Because it affects the lobes of the brain that are responsible for judgment and social behavior, frontotemporal dementia can result in impolite and socially inappropriate behavior. Symptoms of this form of dementia usually appear in younger people between the ages of 40 and 65. The disease seems to run in families.

Huntington's disease. Symptoms of this hereditary disorder typically begin between the ages of 30 and 50, starting with mild personality changes. As the disorder progresses, a person with Huntington's develops involuntary jerky movements, muscle weakness and clumsiness. Dementia commonly develops in the later stages of the disease.

Parkinson's disease. People with Parkinson's disease may experience stiffness of limbs, shaking at rest (tremor), speech impairment and a shuffling gait. About 10 percent of people with Parkinson's develop dementia late in the disease.

Creutzfeldt-Jakob disease. This extremely rare and fatal brain disorder belongs to a family of human and animal diseases known as the transmissible spongiform encephalopathies. A new variety of Creutzfeldt-Jakob disease has emerged—particularly in Britain. It's believed to be linked to the human consumption of beef from cattle with mad cow disease (bovine spongiform encephalopathy).

DIAGNOSIS

Alzheimer's disease and most types of dementia can only be definitely diagnosed by the presence of microscopic changes in the brain— something that is not possible while the patient is alive unless a brain biopsy is performed.

This is why doctors usually diagnose patients who exhibit the classic symptoms of AD with "possible" Alzheimer's or "probable" Alzheimer's. Other forms of dementia are diagnosed by paying particular attention to characteristic symptoms that give strong clues. At specialized centers, doctors can correctly diagnose AD about 90 percent of the time based on several tools:

- Questions about the person's general health, past medical problems and ability to carry out daily activities.
- Tests to measure memory, problem solving, attention, counting and language.
- Medical tests, such as tests of blood, urine, or spinal fluid and brain scans.

• PET (positron emission tomography) scanning is increasingly becoming an important tool in the diagnosis of AD. In a study published in the *New England Journal of Medicine* in December 2006, PET scans were able to differentiate between people with probable AD as opposed to those with mild cognitive impairment (MCI).

Early and accurate diagnosis of AD or other types of dementia is important for patients and families. I'll discuss ways of slowing the progression of the disease in the coming chapters, but it's important to know here that the earlier you start, the better results the patient may get from diet, exercise and supplement programs.

An early diagnosis can also provide the time to discuss care options and the patient's wishes while they are still able to take part in making decisions.

CONVENTIONAL TREATMENTS

There is no cure for Alzheimer's or any of the other forms of dementia I've mentioned in this chapter.

However, there are treatments used by conventional medicine that have varying degrees of effect depending on the stage to which the disease has progressed.

In recent years, several pharmaceuticals that target the symptoms of AD and dementia have come on the market. In my experience, they are only minimally effective particularly if AD has reached the moderate or severe stage.

The drugs that are commonly used fall into two categories:
• Those that address the symptoms of mild and moderate AD and may or may not slow the progression of the disease.
• Those that address the behavioral problems that usually occur as the disease worsens.

Cholinesterase inhibitors
The first Alzheimer's medications to be approved were cholinesterase inhibitors.

Three of these drugs are commonly prescribed:
• donepezil (Aricept®)
• rivastigmine (Exelon®)
• and galantamine, approved under the trade name Reminyl® and renamed Razadyne® in 2005.

These drugs are designed to prevent the breakdown of acetylcholine, a chemical messenger in the brain that is important for memory and other thinking skills. The drugs are intended to keep levels of the chemical messenger high, even while the cells that produce the messenger continue to become damaged or die. About half of the people who take cholinesterase inhibitors initially experience a mild to modest improvement in cognitive symptoms.

Aricept™ (donepezil)

This drug is probably the most widely known pharmaceutical to treat symptoms of Alzheimer's, probably because of the massive television advertising campaign by the manufacturer.

Aricept™ was approved by the FDA for the treatment of mild to moderate AD in 1996 and for severe AD in 2006.

While Aricept™ doesn't have any severe side effects, I don't find it particularly effective for the long term. Some families have heard about it and ask for a prescription because they feel like they need to be doing something to help Grandma or Grandpa. I'm happy to comply, but I warn them that the drug is unlikely to make a dramatic difference and, if there is improvement, it is likely to be relatively temporary.

Namenda™ (memantine)

Namenda™ is designed to enhance the brain's production of glutamate, a brain chemical associated with learning and memory. Patients with AD usually have low levels of glutamate, so this drug is designed to restore that function.

One of the side effects of Namenda™ is increased confusion when someone first starts taking the drug. This confusion usually improves over time.

Namenda™ is not effective for all patients and the improvements, if any, are usually small. Improvements should be noticeable within a few weeks.

BEHAVIORAL TREATMENTS

If psychiatric symptoms accompany the dementia, drug therapies may include:

Antidepressant medications for low mood and irritability
• citalopram (Celexa®)
• fluoxetine (Prozac®)
• paroxetine (Paxil®)
• sertraline (Zoloft®)

Anxiolytics for anxiety, restlessness, verbally disruptive behavior and resistance
• lorazepam (Ativan®)
• oxazepam (Serax®)

Antipsychotic medications for hallucinations, delusions, aggression, hostility and uncooperativeness
• aripiprazole (Abilify®)
• clozapine (Clozaril®)

- olanzapine (Zyprexa®)
- quetiapine (Seroquel®)
- risperidone (Risperdal®)
- ziprasidone (Geodon®)

Although antipsychotics are among the most frequently used medications for treating agitation, some physicians may prescribe an anticonvulsant/mood stabilizer, such as carbamazepine (Tegretol®) or divalproex (Depakote®) for hostility or aggression.

OTHER DIAGNOSES

I know I've said it before, but I'll keep apologizing for the grim nature and the bleak prognosis for patients with dementia and for their families. There is no cure and there is no effective treatment for these devastating diseases. It may take many years of complete caregiving before the patient inevitably dies. There is no way to sugar coat it.

However, there is some hope. Not all forms of dementia are what they appear to be. Experts estimate that about 10 to 15 percent of all dementia is caused by reversible conditions. Some of these conditions appear to be dementia, but the symptoms are caused by identifiable and treatable conditions.

That's why a detailed diagnostic procedure should be undertaken by anyone exhibiting the many symptoms identified in this chapter.

Among them are:

Pseudo dementia: This is actually a form of depression that can cause memory loss and appears much like mild Alzheimer's. In fact, some experts estimate that as many as one-third of people initially diagnosed with Alzheimer's may actually be suffering from treatable pseudo dementia.

The patient is inattentive to his surroundings and is usually very conscious of the problem, but seems to be incapable of rectifying the situation. The slowness and apathy mimic Alzheimer's, but he may also display other symptoms of depression, including irritability, lack of energy, loss of ability to concentrate, insomnia (usually awakening early), loss of appetite with weight loss and constipation, unwillingness to engage in conversation, appearance of sadness, feelings of guilt or low self-esteem and thoughts of suicide.

To be diagnosed with pseudo dementia requires only some of these symptoms and, to be honest, it's sometimes just a guess on my part.

One major clue for me is that the patient usually comes to my office alone, expressing concern about the symptoms, rather than being brought in by family members.

The symptoms usually disappear when the patient is treated with antidepressants. Remember that depression is caused by an imbalance of neurotransmitters or brain chemicals. There is no stigma to being treated for this disease and treatments are often very successful. This is the most treatable of the diseases that mimic AD or dementia.

If I suspect in any way that a patient's problem may be pseudo dementia, I'll prescribe a few weeks of anti-depressants to see if we get improvement.

Vitamin B12 deficiency (also known as Subacute Combined Degeneration): Shortfalls of B12 can cause nerve damage, particularly in people older than 60. Alcoholics are at particularly high risk of B12 deficiency. Symptoms of this rare condition can include difficulty walking, confusion, irritability and mild depression. In severe cases, B12 deficiency may cause delirium, paranoia and impaired mental function. B12 deficiency is diagnosed with a simple blood test and the condition can be significantly improved with B12 injections.

Brain tumors: These can be removed surgically.

Extreme hypothyroidism: Among the many symptoms of low thyroid function are depression, difficulty in concentrating and memory impairment. However, as we've seen just from the symptoms described in this chapter, these can also be symptoms of AD as well as several other diseases. Hypothyroidism is very common in postmenopausal women. Detailed testing of thyroid function can produce a diagnosis, and standard pharmaceuticals to treat low thyroid function usually reverse all the symptoms.

Syphilis: The late stages of this sexually transmitted disease include insanity. At one time, untreated syphilis was a significant cause of memory impairment, but it is uncommon today because antibiotics have made treatment of syphilis a simple process. However, when syphilis goes untreated, it can affect brain cells. Syphilis can be diagnosed by testing blood and sometimes spinal fluid. If it is confirmed, an intensive month-long course of penicillin will cure the infection, but residual damage may be permanent.

Reactions to medications: Some medications have side effects that mimic the symptoms of dementia. A single medicine may trigger such a reaction in an older person or in someone who has a long-term debilitating illness. Stopping the medication will reverse the problem.

Infections: Meningitis and encephalitis, which are infections of the nervous system, can cause memory loss or sudden dementia. Treating the infection can reverse the situation.

Normal-pressure hydrocephalus (NPH): When cerebrospinal fluid builds up in the ventricles of the brain, the brain tissue is compressed even though the fluid pressure remains normal. This may cause dementia along with a unique gait difficulty and urinary incontinence. If this condition is identified in time, it may be treated by draining the excess fluid via a tube leading into the abdomen. Return of function can be quite variable.

Toxic reactions to illicit drugs and alcohol abuse: These symptoms can usually be reversed by treating the addiction.

Chemotherapy drugs used to treat various types of cancer: These powerful medications can cause reactions in the brain that affect memory, concentration, planning and problem-solving ability. These usually resolve themselves three or four years after treatment.

IN CONCLUSION

This is a primer about AD and dementia. It's not meant to tell you everything you need to know about the disease or what to expect. In each person diagnosed with any of these diseases, the progression is different, but the eventual outcome is inevitable.

I strongly urge you to seek support if you are a caregiver for someone with AD or dementia. You'll need it. And you have my profound sympathy.

References:

Web sites:

Alzheimer's Association
www.alz.org

National Institute of Neurological Disorders and Stroke
http://www.nia.nih.gov/Alzheimers/Publications/adfact.htm

National Institute on Aging:
http://www.ninds.nih.gov/disorders/alzheimersdisease/
alzheimersdisease.htm

Scientific References:

Mosconi L, Herholz K et al. Metabolic interaction between ApoE genotype and onset age in Alzheimer's disease: implications for brain reserve. Journal of Neurology, Neurosurgery and Psychiatry 2005 Jan;76(1):15-23.

White AR, Huang X et al. Homocysteine potentiates copper- and amyloid beta peptide-mediated toxicity in primary neuronal cultures: possible risk factors in the Alzheimer's-type neurodegenerative pathways. Journal of Neurochemistry 2001 Mar;76(5):1509-20.

Seman LJ, McNamara JR, et al. Lipoprotein(a), Homocysteine, and remnant like particles: emerging risk factors. Current Opinions in Cardiology 1999;14:186-91.

Lalouschek W, Aull S, et al. Genetic and nongenetic factors influencing plasma homocysteine levels in patients with ischemic cerebrovascular disease and in healthy control subjects. Journal of Laboratory and Clinical Medicine 1999;133:575-82.

Tucker KL, Ning Q et al. High homocysteine and low B vitamins predict cognitive decline in aging men: the Veterans Affairs Normative Aging Study. American Journal of Clinical Nutrition Sep 2005;82:627- 635.

Ravaglia G, Fort P et al. Homocysteine and folate as risk factors for dementia and Alzheimer disease. American Journal of Clinical Nutrition Sep 2005;82:636-643.

Lautenschlager T, Flicker L et al. Subjective Memory Complaints With and Without Objective Memory Impairment: Relationship With Risk Factors for Dementia. American Journal of Geriatric Psychiatry Aug 2005;13:731-734.

Kruman, II, Mouton CA, et al. Folate deficiency inhibits proliferation of adult hippocampal progenitors. Neuroreport 2005 Jul 13;16(10):1055-1059.

Wouters-Wesseling W, Wagenaar LW et al. Effect of an enriched drink on cognitive function in frail elderly persons. Journal of Gerontology 2005 60:265-270.

Glueck CJ, Shaw P et al. *Evidence that homocysteine is an independent risk factor for atherosclerosis in hyperlipidemic patients.* American Journal of Cardiology 1995;75:132-6.

Ubbink JB, Vermaak WJH et al. *Vitamin B12, vitamin B6, and folate nutritional status in men with hyperhomocysteinemia.* American Journal of Clinical Nutrition 1993;57:47-53.

Ubbink JB, Vermaak WJH, et al. *Vitamin requirements for the treatment of hyperhomocysteinemia in humans.* Journal of Nutrition 1994;124:1927-33.

Wilcken DEL, Wilcken B et al. *Homocysteinuria-the effects of betaine in the treatment of patients not responsive to pyridoxine.* New England Journal of Medicine 1983;309:448-53.

Fava M, Rosenbaum JF et al. *Neuroendocrine effects of S-adenosyl-L-methionine, a novel putative antidepressant.* Journal of Psychiatric Research 1990;24:177-84.

Schumacher HR. *Osteoarthritis: The clinical picture, pathogenesis, and management with studies on a new therapeutic agent, S-adenosylmethionine.* American Journal of Medicine 1987;83(suppl 5A):1-4.

Osman E, Owen JS, Burroughs AK. *S-adenosyl-L-methionine-a new therapeutic agent in liver disease?* Alimentary Pharmacology and Therapeutics 1993;7:21-8.

Gatto G, Caleri D et al. *Analgesizing effect of a methyl donor (S-adenosylmethionine) in migraine: an open clinical trial.* International Journal of Pharmacology Research 1986;6:15-7.

Tavoni A, Jeracitano G et al. *Evaluation of S-adenosylmethionine in secondary fibromyalgia: a double-blind study.* Clinical and Experimental Rheumatology 1998;16:106-7.

Liou HH, Tsai MC et al. *Environmental risk factors and Parkinson's disease: a case-control study in Taiwan.* Neurology 1997;48:1583-1588.

Goldsmith JR, Herishanu Y et al. *Clustering of Parkinson's disease points to environmental etiology.* Archives of Environmental Health 1990;45:88-94.

Semchuk KM, Love EJ et al. *Parkinson's disease and exposure to agricultural work and pesticide chemicals.* Neurology 1992;42:1328-1335.

Bartzokis G, Sultzer D. *In vivo evaluation of brain iron in Alzheimer's disease and normal subjects using MRI.* Biological Psychiatry 1994 Apr 1;35(7);480-7.

Haupt M, Kurz A. *Reversibility of dementia in hypothyroidism.* Zeitschrift für die gesamte innere Medizin und ihre Grenzgebiete 1993 Dec;48(12):609-13.

Inagaki M, Yoshikawa E et al. *Smaller regional volumes of brain gray and white matter demonstrated in breast cancer survivors exposed to adjuvant chemotherapy.* Cancer 2007 Jan 1;109(1):146-56.

Small GW, Kepe V et al. *PET of brain amyloid and tau in mild cognitive impairment.* New England Journal of Medicine 2006 Dec 21;355(25);2562-62.

Are You at Risk?

Families of my Alzheimer's and dementia patients invariably want to know two things: First, they want to know their chances of developing the diseases and, second, regardless of their risk level, they want to know how to diminish the possibility they will someday become victims of these devastating diseases.

As there are no guarantees in life, there is no 100% certain way to determine your risk, but there is a broad body of scientific evidence that gives an idea of who is at highest risk and the factors that have been shown to help neutralize that risk.

You cannot control some of the biggest risk factors such as family history and age. But you have a great deal of control over other risk factors that can make a huge difference in your ability to prevent the disease entirely, delay the onset or diminish the effects if you've already experienced some cognitive impairment. We'll talk about these in detail in future chapters.

RISK FACTOR SURVEY

I've devised this basic questionnaire based on scientific evidence that certain factors affect your risk of Alzheimer's disease and dementia. I've attached general point values to the questions in rough approximation of the increased or decreased risk a certain trait or behavior might have. For example, we know there is research that shows that smoking increases your risk of AD by 250%.

While this survey is based on scientific evidence, this survey isn't precisely scientific and should be viewed in broad terms.

By answering the following questions, you can get a good idea of the risk factors you carry for AD and dementia. Knowing where you stand in terms of risk can help you to take the preventive measures that can delay or even prevent the onset of AD before symptoms begin to appear.

RISK QUESTIONNAIRE

1. Do you have a grandmother or grandfather with AD or dementia?
   Yes (3)   No (0)

2. Do you have a parent with AD or dementia?
   Yes (3)   No (0)

3. Do you have a sister or brother with AD or dementia?
   Yes (3)   No (0)

4. How old are you?
   18-35 ....0 points
   36-60 ....1 point
   61-65 ....2 points
   66-75 ....3 points
   76-85 ....4 points
   86+ ....6 points

5. Have you been diagnosed with any of the following diseases?
   diabetes ....3 points
   heart disease....................................3 points
   stroke ....4 points
   Parkinson's disease...........................4 points
   high blood pressure ....2 points
   HIV/AIDS...2 points
   multiple sclerosis ....2 points
   thyroid disease..................................1 point
   anemia...1 point
   depression ....1 point

6. What is your level of education?
   Graduate degree................................0 points
   College degree ....0 points
   High school diploma..........................1 point
   GED...1 point
   Elementary school only ....3 points

7. Do you smoke?
   Yes (2)   No (0)

8. Do you drink wine?
   Yes   No (0)
   If yes, how much?
   Less than 1 glass* a day.....................0 points
   2-3 glasses a day...............................-2 points
   4 or more..3 points
   *1 glass = 5 ounces

9. Are you overweight?
    Yes   No (0)
    If yes, by how much?
    Less than 30 pounds ....0 points
    30-50 pounds ....1 point
    50 pounds or more ....2 points

10. Does your diet include lots of meat and fatty foods?
    Yes (2) No (0)

11. Do you eat fish or take a fish oil supplement?
    Yes (-2) No (2)

12. Do you exercise regularly? (At least 30 minutes of vigorous exercise at least three times a week)
    Yes (-2) No (2)

13. Do you engage in mental challenges and regularly learn new things?
    Yes (-4) No (4)

14. Do you regularly socialize with a group of friends or family?
    Yes (-2) No (2)

15. Have you ever had head injury or brain trauma?
    Yes (2)   No (0)

16. Have you ever lived on a farm or had extensive exposure to agricultural chemicals?
    Yes (2)   No (0)

17. What is your homocysteine level?
    Over 15...2 points
    Under 12 ....0 points
    Don't know ....1 point

Score yourself as follows:

If your score is 10 points or more, you are at risk for AD and dementia, and you should begin implementing the preventive measures outlined in Chapter 5 and consider the supplements in Chapter 8.

If your score is 15 points or more, you are at high risk and you should immediately being a preventive program that may include pharmaceuticals.

As you can see, there are some risk factors over which you have no control such as age and family history.

With other factors, you may have only minimal control, such as whether or not you lived on a farm or had childhood diabetes, developed one of the high-risk diseases like MS or Parkinson's or had a brain injury.

But, you'll also be able to see that the vast majority of the risk factors are well within your control.

You can control your diet, eat lots of antioxidant-rich fruits and vegetables and healthy fats.

You can control your weight to prevent Type 2 diabetes and hypertension.

You can choose not to smoke or drink alcohol excessively. You can choose to exercise your body and mind.

You can participate in social activities with family and friends.

You can choose to exercise your body in any way that you enjoy.

You can choose to exercise your mind regardless of your level of education.

This chapter promises you a deeper look at the risks and offers the means of neutralizing them.

The goal is to delay the onset of Alzheimer's or prevent it altogether.

For anyone who has watched a loved one slip away in the fog of AD or dementia, every moment of lucidity is precious. For every moment that you can keep away the demons of dementia, your life and the lives of those you love with be richer. It is within your grasp.

References:

Battanco-Quintana JL, Allam MF et al. Risk factors for Alzheimer's disease, Zeitschrift für die gesamte innere Medizin und ihre Grenzgebiete. 2005 May 16-31;40(10):613-8.

Stampfer MJ. Cardiovascular disease and Alzheimer's disease: common links. Journal of Internal Medicine 2006 Sep;260(3):211-23.

Hu G, Jousilahti P et al. Type 2 diabetes and the risk of Parkinson's disease. Diabetes Care 2007 Apr;30(4):842-7.

Whitmer RA, Gunderson EP et al. Obesity in middle age and future risk of dementia: a 27 year longitudinal population based study. British Medical Journal 2005 Jun 11;330:1360.

Kivipelto M, Gandu T et al. Obesity and vascular risk factors at midlife and the risk of dementia and Alzheimer disease. Archives of Neurology 2005 Oct;62(10);1556-60.

Ott A, Slooter AJ. Smoking and risk of dementia and Alzheimer's disease in a population-based cohort study: the Rotterdam Study. Lancet 1998 Jun 20;351(9119);1840-3.

Aggarwal NT, Bienias JL et al. The relation of cigarette smoking to incident Alzheimer's disease in biracial urban community population. Neuroepidemiology 2006;26(3);140-6.

Rovio S, Karehjolt I et al. Leisure time physical activity at midlife and the risk of dementia and Alzheimer's disease. Lancet Neurology 2005 Nov;4(11);705-11.

Pinder RM, Sandler M. Alcohol, wine and mental health; focus on dementia and stroke. Journal of Psychopharmacology 2004 Dec;18(4);449-56.

Luchsinger Ja, Tang MX et al. Alcohol intake and risk of dementia. Journal of the American Geriatric Society;52(4);540-6.

Vogel T, Benetos A. Rick factors for Alzheimer: towards prevention? Presse Med 2006 Sep;35(9 Pt 2);1309-16.

Deng J, Zhou DH et al. A 2-year follow-up study of alcohol consumption and risk of dementia. Clinical Neurology and Neruosurgery 2006 Jun;108(4):378-83.

Laitinen MH, Ngandu T et al. Fat intake at mid life and risk of dementia and Alzheimer's disease: a population-based study. Dementia and Geriatric Cognitive Disorders 2006;22(1);99-107.

Cole GM, Frautschy SA. Docosahexaenoic acid protects from amyloid and dendritic pathology in an Alzheimer's disease mouse model. Nutritional Health 2006;18(3):249-59.

How to Prevent Memory Loss

Now you have all the information you need. You know how your brain and memory work, you know your risks and you know all the grim details of Alzheimer's and other forms of dementia.

Now we can get to the positive aspect of things: How you can preserve your brain function, prevent Alzheimer's and dementia or, if you do at some time experience memory impairment, how you can delay or minimize the effects of the disease.

Now it's time to take action.

I'm going to address mental and physical exercise, sleep, stress management and mental attitude in this chapter and extensively look at the diet and the right supplements in Chapters 7 and 8.

But there is one piece of advice I can give you that is more important than any of the rest. It' simple:

If you want to keep your memory, use it.

DON'T LOSE YOUR MIND

None of us wants to lose our minds, literally or figuratively.

If you want to keep your memory, make it your lifelong mission to stimulate your mind as much as possible.

You'll remember from Chapter 2 that each neuron grows root-like extensions called dendrites through which thoughts travel as electrical impulses.

The more of these neural pathways you are able to forge throughout your life, the more brain reserve you will have and the stronger your memory will be, whether or not you ever develop any type of dementia.

Think of it as a fail-safe net. If, at some time in your future, you develop AD or dementia and the disease begins to damage your memory pathways and other areas of your brain, the existence of hundreds, thousands and even millions of alternate pathways for these messages to travel can minimize the effects of the memory loss.

Mental stimulation is the only way we know to extend and strengthen that network.

In the Nun Study, Dr. David Snowdon found three powerful messages.

The first was simple one: Those with college degrees had a much better chance of surviving to old age and maintaining their independence.

Second, by looking at autobiographies written by young women who entered the sisterhood of Notre Dame, Dr. Snowdon could very accurately predict who would become cognitively impaired 50 or 60 years later. No, he isn't psychic. He used an elaborate method of screening these essays for "idea density" and grammatical complexity. Those young women who, in their early 20s, expressed the most complex thought patterns, i.e., those who were using their brains the most, were far less likely to suffer from cognitive impairment late in life.

Finally, what seems to make the difference is the level of active mental engagement these women invested throughout their lives. One octogenarian told Dr. Snowdon she was far too busy to participate in his study because she had just completed an advanced degree and was about to leave for a missionary assignment in Africa!

What's more, even some people the age of 100 or more are still able to learn and do new things. Researchers at Beth Israel Deaconess Hospital in Boston attributed this to their determination to remain mentally active even in extreme old age.

In a 2002 paper, those researchers cited two remarkable older people with brain reserves that served them well:

"J.L. did not have much formal education, but she elected to have cataract surgery in her 90s because reading was so important to her, and at 103, she still read constantly. She continued to make major decisions in the family and balance her checkbook without a calculator. Another possible protective factor was her living situation: she had resided in the same apartment for many years, living independently, with a grandson in the same apartment and a daughter a block away.

"Similarly, L.B.L. continued to engage in challenging activities, teaching her paralyzed hand to function during the last few months of her life. She had taken up painting in oils and watercolors in her 90s and, like J.L., was an avid reader. At age 100, she wrote a book about her experiences in the Holocaust and gave a speech on the subject in front of a large group."

THE BRAIN CHALLENGE

There are many ways to challenge your brain. Choose among the ones that appeal to you. Be sure to choose several so you don't get stuck in a rut. You want to stimulate as many areas of your brain as possible.

Here are the best:

- **Learn anything new.** It almost goes without saying that stimulating any part of your brain where you haven't already developed reserves will serve you well and prevent cognitive decline. Be a regular at adult education classes. Go for that master's degree you've always wanted. Teach a class that requires you to learn something new. It doesn't matter so much what you do; it's more important that you are doing something.

- **Learn a foreign language.** This stimulates you to think in a way you might not ordinarily think, increasing your brain reserves. A recent study noted that by using a second language you can delay onset of dementia by four years.
- **Work sudoku or crossword puzzles.** The latest mathematical rage stimulates the left side of the brain that governs logical and mathematical functions. Crossword puzzles have similar effects stimulating vocabulary-related areas of the brain as well as requiring some mathematical calculations.
- **Take up ballroom dancing.** I'll talk more about the importance of exercise and socializing later in this chapter, but let it suffice to say that encouraging your brain to memorize new steps and movements enhances the development of new neural pathways. It doesn't have to be ballroom dancing. Try line dancing, square dancing, folk dancing or any other structured type of dancing that requires you to memorize the movements.
- **Play board games or card games.** Not only is this a wonderful social activity, it stimulates the thinking and strategic brain pathways.
- **Read a book**, then join a book club. I think reading is great, but it only goes so far if you don't retain what you are reading. It's better to read a book and then discuss it with others.
- **Learn a new computer operating system.** I really liked this suggestion from Drs. Andrew Weil and Gary Small in *The Healthy Brain*. Their contention that forcing your brain to do something completely unfamiliar and somewhat uncomfortable is excellent mental stimulation.
- **Learn to play a musical instrument.** Chinese researchers found that people who know how to play a musical instrument are able to remember a list of words better than non-musical types. The scientists think that learning music gives you two important areas of stimulation: it activates the left temporal lobe of the brain, which processes auditory input, and simultaneously encourages the development of an adjacent lobe of the brain which is responsible for verbal memory.
- **Play computer games.** An interesting small study recently showed that even people with mild Alzheimer's were able to improve their mental condition when they played computer games, probably because they were stimulating new parts of their brains and developing new brain reserves even as their existing neural pathways were being destroyed by the disease. Encourage your children and grandchildren to play video games (within limits, of course) and play with them. Braden Allenby, a professor at Arizona State University, found marked differences

between the MRIs of brains of young people who play video games and older people who are video game abstainers. It seems these computer whiz kids are forging a whole new set of mental and physical abilities requiring hand-eye coordination not seen in older generations.

- **Switch sides of your brain.** If you have spent a good part of your day performing rote and repetitive tasks, like weeding the garden, take a few minutes to write in your journal or work a sudoku. Conversely, if you've been writing or reading for a few hours, stop and file your papers, sweep the floor or do some such repetitive task to balance the stimulation of the hemispheres of your brain.

Any passive activities can impair your cognitive function or, at the very least, don't stimulate brain function.

Watching TV is probably the worst. Researchers have found that people who watch television more than an hour or so a day are at a higher risk of cognitive impairment. It makes a difference what kind of TV you watch. A study from the City University of New York showed that women who watched daytime television, particularly soap operas and talk shows, scored poorly on tests of memory, attention and other cognitive skills. Television watching is passive and fairly mindless. Use your time on more productive activities.

The absolute worst thing you can do for your body, mind and spirit is to become a couch potato and just hang out all day, doing nothing in particular.

If you've always loved knitting or woodworking or dog training, by all means continue to participate in these activities, but what's most important is that you challenge yourself to learn new things and take your mind in new directions.

THE BODY CHALLENGE

Physical exercise is essential to good health at all ages. As your years pass, physical exercise is almost as important as mental exercise in preventing cognitive decline.

Think about it. It stands to reason that the more you move your body and oxygenate your system, the more vital your mental function will be.

Exercise also reduces stress hormones and increases the production of neurotransmitters, nourishing the brain cells and helping reduce the risk of depression and other types of damage to brain cells.

Countless studies show that exercise plays a key role in preventing many of the conditions that lead to a high risk of dementia, including heart disease, stroke and diabetes.

One really interesting British study showed that if a child is physically fit at the age of 11, this will predict good cognitive function at the age of 79;

so it's important to encourage your children and grandchildren to be fit.

That doesn't mean you have to train for a marathon. In fact, a simple half-hour walk three times a week will do wonders for your heart and your brain. If you prefer, gardening is an excellent way of working out all muscle groups, getting fit and improving mood.

It's never too late to begin your exercise program. Dr. Snowdon tells the story of a delightful nun, Sister Nicolette, who outlived all her classmates. Her secret? She walked several miles a day—but she didn't begin until age 70!

Regular exercise will also keep your heart, lungs and bones strong, improving your odds for a healthy old age.

I recommend that you choose a form of exercise you love and stick with it. You might enjoy a Tai Chi class, which has the added benefits of helping improve balance and reducing the risk of falls. Maybe tennis is your thing. By all means, go for it!

It doesn't matter what you do, it's that you do it regularly. Exercise should be fun. If you enjoy your exercise program and look forward to it, you'll be far more likely to stick with it. If you see it as a chore, look for another form of exercise that is more enjoyable for you.

DR. JOSEPHS' 30-DAY CHALLENGE TO JUMP-START YOUR BRAIN

Use it or you'll lose it. That's the simplest advice I can give you if you want to preserve your memory into extreme old age. Challenge your brain every day, grit your teeth and force yourself to learn new things and take in new experiences and it will serve you well at any stage in life. Challenge your body as well and keep yourself fit and keep the blood and oxygen circulating through your brain for optimum brain health.

This is a two-part challenge for mental and physical fitness. I know there is a lot here and if you are still working and have family responsibilities, you may have to modify it to fit your lifestyle. If you're still working and have family responsibilities, you're probably getting quite a bit of stimulation anyway. This is a jump-start. You'll find your life will change rather dramatically if you can do all these things. Do as much as you can.

Day 1: Buy yourself a sudoku book. Take a five-minute walk.

Day 2: Do at least one soduku puzzle. It doesn't matter if you get it right, you're still challenging your brain.
Buy yourself a set of hand weights in 1-, 2-3 and 5-pound capacities. They're cheap, and shouldn't cost more than $20. If money is really a problem you can use a water bottle or milk jugs filled with water.

Day 3: Get a younger person to show you how to play a video game.

Take another five-minute walk and spend five more minutes with simple exercises with the hand weights. If you're not familiar with these exercises, you can find them and print out diagrams in a book called *Fitness After Fifty* by Wayne Westcott and Thomas Baechle, or *Strength Training for Beginners* by Susie Dinan and Joan Bassey.

Day 4: Play a video game. If anyone you know has the Wii video game, play a round of tennis or try swordfighting with the computer images. It's fun!

Day 5: Check out book clubs in your area. Join one. Take a 10-minute walk today, longer if you like.

Day 6: Start reading the book club selection for the next meeting. Today's a good day for ten minutes of strength training. Remember to go slowly and not strain.

Day 7: Work a crossword puzzle. Play frisbee with your dog (or the neighbor's dog) for at least 15 minutes. If there is no dog partner available, think of some other form of exercise that is fun for you.

Day 8: Does your community college or similar venue offer ballroom dancing? How about a local club that teaches line dancing or square dancing? Gather information. Walk ten minutes. Pick up the pace just a little.

Day 9: Decide which dance class you'd like to take. Sign up. Ready for another Wii session? It's so much fun, you may decide to buy your own.

Day 10: Do at least two more sudoku puzzles. You may already be addicted by now. Strength training today for 15 minutes.

Day 11: Finish reading your book club book. Take notes for the discussion. Walk 20 minutes today. Do intervals, sometimes walking faster, sometimes strolling. Just keep moving!

Day 12: Put on your dancing shoes and go to dance class.
The dancing may fill both your physical and your mental needs today. Do some gentle yoga stretching to help you warm up. If you're not familiar with yoga, get a copy of *Yoga for All of Us: A Modified Series of Traditional Poses for Any Age and Ability* by Peggy Cappy, or The American Yoga Association's *Easy Does It Yoga: The Safe and Gentle Way to Health and Well-Being* by Alice Christensen.

Day 13: Haven't you always wanted to learn to speak Chinese or Russian? Find out where you can take a foreign language class. Sign up. Strength training today for 15 minutes.

Day 14: Attend your book club meeting. Actively engage in the discussion. Walk today. Do your 20 minutes with vigor. Take a new route.

Day 15: Do you have a computer? If not, ask a family member to teach you the basics. If you do, try out a program you've never used before, like Excel. Today's Wii day or yoga or frisbee. What's most fun for you? Do it for at least 30 minutes.

Day 16: Still doing Sudoku? You're probably ready to move to a more difficult level. Do that and do a crossword today. Another walking day. Can you do 20 minutes? Try walking forward for five minutes and backward for one minute and then repeat.

Day 17: Have you bought the next book club selection? Do it today and start reading. Have you found a walking buddy yet? If not, do that today and go out for 20 minutes of slow and fast walking.

Day 18: Have you practiced your new dance moves? Do so today. Before your dance practice, do 10 minutes of gentle yoga stretching.

Day 19: Start language class today. Strength training day. If you're not feeling challenged, bump up the weight one pound.

Day 20: Do more sudoku and crosswords. Practice your yoga stretching and your dance steps for 15 minutes.

Day 21: Play a rowdy game of Monopoly or Scrabble with friends or family. Laugh a lot. This is a good day for Wii or other fun exercise. Can you get in 30 minutes?

Day 22: How's your foreign language practice going? Work on it today. Maybe you can practice with someone in your class. You can even combine it with today's exercise assignment. Today take a brisk walk to a specific destination: a friend's house, the coffee shop, somewhere you like to go. Walk back home.

Day 23: How are your new computer skills developing? Keep working on them. Ask for help if you need it. This is a good day for strength training. Put on some upbeat music and try for 20 vigorous minutes.

Day 24: Played any video games lately? How are your dance skills going? Do both of these today. They count for mental and physical exercise.

Day 25: Go to dance class or, better yet, plan an evening of dancing somewhere. Be sure to do a little yoga before you put on your dancing shoes so you'll be well limbered up.

Day 26: Have you finished your book club selection yet? Talk to a friend about the book you've read. Walk with your buddy for 20 minutes. Pick up the pace just a bit. Can you do a mile in 20 minutes? It's a good goal to set.

Day 27: How's that Chinese grammar coming along? Why not contact a classmate and try out some of your newfound language skills? This is a good day for fun exercise. Break out the Wii or the frisbee and have fun. Laugh—it's great aerobic exercise.

Day 28: You must be a sudoku master by now! Buy another book at a higher level and promise yourself you'll do at least one sudoku a day. Challenge yourself to a timed race with somebody younger and see who finishes the puzzle first. Strength training today for 20 minutes. You're getting stronger and so are your bones, and your brain!

Day 29: Your computer is calling you. Try something you've never done before. Create a database for your Christmas card list, create a card for a friend with clip art or look for your house as seen by satellite by going to www.maps.google.com.

Day 30: This is a good day for dancing. Try out those new dance steps with a partner. As always, use your exercise today for gentle yoga or tai chi warm-ups before you dance. It'll keep the dancing fun and strain free. Your muscles will thank you.

A FEW HINTS:

(1) These are basic recommendations. If it's the middle of the winter and it's too icy to walk outside, consider walking around the mall or around the gym at your local high school. Get a buddy to walk with you. It's much more fun that way and you'll be less likely to slack off. There are even mall walking clubs you can join. If you don't have a dog to play Frisbee with or you don't know anybody who has Wii, get creative. Ride a bike, sign up for a tai chi class, get one of those huge exercise balls and bounce away or go for a few laps in the local pool. Do something different on these days so your exercise program doesn't become monotonous. Have fun!

(2) I'm asking you to take a lot of classes. Many of these will be available through your local community college and they may be free if you're over 60. The same thing holds true for recommended books. If you don't want to buy them, you'll probably find them at your local library.

(3) I know, it seems like this will be very time consuming. It actually isn't bad on a daily basis. Nothing will take more than an hour. Yes, you'll be out several nights a week learning Chinese or taking a yoga class or attending your book club meeting, but since you won't be vegging out in front of the TV, you'll have plenty of time. Bring the family or a friend along. The more the merrier!

GET A (SOCIAL) LIFE

It stands to reason that if an older person is isolated from family and friends, mental function might be compromised, whether or not the person has Alzheimer's or dementia. After all, if you haven't got anyone to talk to and no one seems to care, you might lose touch with the outer world.

There are lots of studies that show that older people who have a large social network of family and friends are less likely to become demented.

I think it is surprising that social interaction throughout life has a positive effect on mental function late in life.

The Honolulu-Asia Aging study looked at the lives of Japanese-American men and their social structures. Late in life, social isolation increased the risk of dementia by nearly two and one-half times; but those who had strong social networks in mid-life, even if those networks were no longer as strong as they had once been, had far less risk of Alzheimer's or dementia.

I don't think we really know why this is true, except perhaps those stimulating conversations and the exposure to the ideas of others helped expand the men's brain reserves and provided those all-important alternative neural pathways later in life.

I think there is something comforting about knowing that family and friends are there for you. We know that cancer patients who are surrounded by family and friends recover more quickly and have fewer risks of recurrence of the cancer, so there is no doubt in my mind that this transfers to the idea that feeling supported is healing, and probably preventive of all types of health problems.

If you don't have much of a social life, make yourself one. Many social activities also help develop brain reserves and provide intellectual and/or physical stimulation, so you get a double effect.

Take a course at the community college. Join a church group or a bridge club. Join a hiking group or take dancing lessons. There are unlimited possibilities of things you can do. Not only will you be getting some social interaction, you'll be stimulating your brain and your body. Find something fun and jump in!

STRESS MANAGEMENT

In the modern world, our lives are filled with stress. No thanks to the Internet, Blackberries, X-Box and hundreds of cable channels, we are never without stimulation and demands made on our time. That long-term unrelieved stress is incredibly damaging to everyone's health.

Cortisol is the well-known stress hormone that is released when we get that "fight-or-flight" response to a stressor. Long-term elevated cortisol suppresses the immune system and can cause chronic inflammation, both of which can open the door for all sorts of degenerative diseases, including heart disease and cancer.

Stress affects every system of your body. There is now scientific evidence that suggests that long-term chronic stress contributes to the deterioration of the hippocampus, the part of the brain where short-term memories are stored. You can see how this can contribute to memory loss.

Since stress is an underlying cause of so many medical conditions, managing your stress is guaranteed to have long-term beneficial effects on your overall health and very specifically on your brain health.

There are many ways to manage your stress, and they all begin with recognizing that you are under stress. Whether you are 20, 30, 40, 50, 60 or more, managing stress is a key to a long and healthy life. Basically, if you're alive and breathing, you are experiencing chronic stress, so just start with the assumption that stress is a health risk for you.

Acknowledging you are under stress may be enough to wake you up to the need to take more time for yourself.

How you do this is as individual as your choice of an exercise program.

Maybe you'll choose to watch funny movies, since we know that laughter is a powerful stress reliever. Maybe yoga or meditation are more your style. Maybe for you it's a long bubble bath, a solitary stroll in nature or a quiet evening with your favorite music. Maybe it's a good phone conversation with your dear friend who lives 1,000 miles away or quiet music when you're stuck in traffic on the freeway. Maybe it's an evening of wild and crazy roller skating at the local rink or a rowdy game of hopscotch with the neighborhood kids. It's your choice. Just choose one or two or ten and do them.

Whenever a patient spends 10 minutes telling me how much he has to do, I know he's stressed. Don't bemoan your stress levels. Do something about them.

GET ENOUGH SLEEP

Sleep is an enigma to medical science. Despite our vast knowledge of the functions of the human body, we still don't know why humans sleep. Yet we do know that sleep is essential to our physical, mental and emotional health.

Experts have varying viewpoints on how much sleep we need, usually ranging from six to eight hours nightly. But no one argues that sleep deprivation stresses all our systems, and the chronic stress of long-term sleep deprivation can be devastating to our health.

Dozens of studies show that sleep deprivation diminishes our abilities to recall lists of words, to do mathematical calculations and to recall faces, not to speak of lowering reaction times.

Yet, research now shows us that sleep has a very specific role in helping us create, store and retain memory.

There is evidence that sleep actually helps forge those all-important neuronal pathways that can re-route memory and thought patterns if the dementia or Alzheimer's damages the brain at a later time.

Lack of sleep may even be a source of false dementia, according to research from the University of Chicago. A report in the medical journal *The Lancet* said that cutting back from the standard eight down to four hours of sleep each night produced striking changes in glucose tolerance and endocrine function that mimicked many of the hallmarks of aging, including memory loss.

Other research suggests that it is deep slow-wave sleep and REM sleep, not the passage of time, that helps implant long-term memories in our brains.

That's plenty of evidence to convince me. I try to get at least seven hours of sleep each night and you should, too.

KEEP A POSITIVE ATTITUDE

In the Nun Study, Dr. Snowdon discovered that the aspiring young nuns who wrote their autobiographies in their early 20s contained another gold mine of information: Those who had a positive outlook on life as young women had a 2.5-fold greater chance of simply being alive 60 years later than those with a more pessimistic outlook.

Conversely, depression is definitely a risk factor for AD and dementia. Recent Danish research showed that people over 65 who suffered from depression for more than two years nearly doubled their risk of AD.

Let me simply say this at this point: Depression is a product of a chemical imbalance in the brain. It's not really a big leap to think that an imbalance of those vital neurotransmitters over an extended period of time can also affect the ability of your neural pathways to function, resulting in impaired memory and learning patterns.

Keeping your thinking patterns positive will definitely have a beneficial effect on your brain and body.

MONITOR YOUR HOMOCYSTEINE

High homocysteine levels have been associated with increased risk of cognitive dysfunction.

We know that high homocysteine levels increase the risk of heart disease, but recent research shows that there is a separate mechanism that increases the risk of Alzheimer's and dementia.

One large Italian study found that elderly people with homocysteine levels over 15 doubled their risk of developing dementia. And there is a Dutch study which showed that frail elderly people who were given vitamin B supplements improved their mental function at the same time they lowered their homocysteine levels.

It is important to have your doctor monitor your levels of blood homocysteine after the age of 40.

I'll address the subject of supplementation in Chapter 8, but I highly recommend B-complex supplements, paying particular attention to folic acid, to lower homocysteine and result in a corresponding reduction in the risk of memory impairment and heart disease. Stubbornly high levels of homocysteine can often successfully be budged with trimethyglycine (TMG) and SAM-e, but more about that later.

DON'T SMOKE

You've heard it a million times and here it goes again: Smoking is perhaps the most dangerous single behavior you can engage in. It will shorten your life. No, I didn't say it "might" or it "may" shorten your life. I said it WILL shorten your life. There is no doubt about it.

Smoking has a strange affect on the human brain. You may even have read something that says smoking is good for your brain.

Nothing could be further from the truth.

But here's the basis of that claim:

Researchers at the Scripps Research Institute found that nornicotine, a byproduct of inhaled nicotine, appears to prevent the buildup of amyloid protein plaques that are characteristic of Alzheimer's.

Logically, that might seem that smoking would protect people against AD.

However, a huge British study on 24,000 doctors debunked that idea and concluded that smoking significantly increases the risk of Alzheimer's and dementia. The researchers aren't sure why this is the case, but I think it probably is connected to the increased risk of other diseases we know that increase the risk of dementia.

So give it up. There is no positive aspect to smoking at all. I won't go into all the details, but I know this is an incredibly difficult addiction to overcome.

I'm absolutely not a fan of excessive pharmaceuticals, but if it takes a month or two of Wellbutrin or other medications that work to help kick the habit, I say go for it. Do whatever you need to do to get that smoking monkey off your back.

CONTROL YOUR BLOOD SUGARS

Scientists have long known that there is a connection between fluctuating blood sugars and memory function. It's really not that surprising since we know that the brain thrives on the sugar in blood. I'm not talking about donuts, I'm talking about the glucose that is the energy engine for the human body, provided by the consumption of complex carbohydrates.

With the upsurge in Type 2 diabetes among people of all ages, we're seeing increased risk factors for impaired memory function. This risk is not only present if you have diabetes, it's present if you have something called IGT or impaired glucose tolerance and even if you have hypoglycemia, which means your blood sugars plummet in the early morning or if you are late for a meal and therefore have increased risk of developing diabetes.

So whatever your status, keep your blood sugars under control. There are two primary ways of accomplishing this:

- First, eliminate simple sugars from your diet. This means you should avoid cakes, pies, candy, sodas, commercial baked goods, table sugar and processed foods. There are many reasons for doing this especially in order to avoid diabetes and the myriad risks for other terrible diseases, including dementia and Alzheimer's.
- The second way to keep the diabetes monster at bay is to exercise regularly. That's another no-brainer since exercise has so many health benefits, it's simply something you should do on a daily basis.

AVOID BRAIN TRAUMA AT ANY AGE

Brain trauma at any age can lead to Alzheimer's or dementia later in life.

While there isn't anything you can do if you have already suffered brain trauma, there is plenty you can do to protect yourself and your children as much as possible right now.

Among them:
- Always wear seat belts.
- Wear helmets when biking, playing football, motorcycling

horseback riding, whitewater rafting or participating in any other sport that carries a risk of head trauma.

- I'm going to be very specific here: Don't box or allow your child to be a boxer. I am anti-boxing because it is not a sport. It is an activity in which the purpose is to knock one's opponent unconscious. It is barbaric and inevitably leads to brain trauma. You only have to look at Muhammed Ali to see the devastating effects of boxing.

IN CONCLUSION

It's not hard to do what you need to do to keep your memory intact and your brain healthy. Eating right, exercising and taking care of your body and mind are the foundations of general overall health.

It needn't take a lot of time or energy. A landmark study from UCLA showed that just 14 days of mental and physical exercises, better diet and stress reduction resulted in improved memory in middle-aged people who reported they were concerned about failing memories.

You can do it too.

Start today. It's not too late.

References:

McEwen, BS. Sleep deprivation as a neurobiologic and physiologic stressor: Allostasis and allostatic load. Metabolism 2006 Oct;55(10 Supple 2):520-3.

Rose CM, Xiong C et al. Education and Alzheimer disease without dementia: support for cognitive reserve hypothesis. Neurology 2007 Jan 16;68(3):223-8.

Mortimer JA, Borenstein AR et al. Very early detection of Alzheimer neuropathology and the role of brain reserve in modifying its clinical expression. Journal of Geriatric Psychiatry and Neurology 2005; 18(4):218-223.

Bialystok E, Craik FI et al. Bilingualism as a protection against the onset of symptoms of dementia. Journal of the International Neuropsychologicl Society 2007 Mar;13(2):209-11.

Snowdon D. Healthy aging and dementia: Findings from the Nun Study. Ann Intern Med. 2003;139:450-454.

Snowdon DA, Greiner LH et al. Linguistic ability in early life and the neuropathology of Alzheimer's disease and cerebrovascular disease: Findings from the Nun Study. Annals of the New York Academy of Sciences 2000:903:34-8.

Deary IJ, Whalley LJ. Physical fitness and lifetime cognitive change. Neurology 2006 Oct 10;67(7):1195-200.

Abbott RD, White LR et al. Walking and dementia in physically capable elderly men. Journal of the American Medical Association 2004;292:1447-1453.

Larson EB, Wang L. Exercise is associated with reduced risk for incident dementia among persons 65 years of age and older. Annals of Internal Medicine 2006 Jan 17;144(2):73-81.

Yu F, Lolanowski AM. Improving cognition and function through exercise intervention in Alzheimer's disease. Journal of Nursing Scholarship 2006;38(4):358-65.

Simons LA, Simons J. Lifestyle factors and risk of dementia: Dubbo Study of the elderly. The Medical Journal of Australia. 2006 Jan 16;(184(2):68-70.

Saczynski JS, Pfeifer LA. The effect of social engagement on incident dementia: the Honolulu-Asia Aging Study. American Journal of Epidemiology 2006 163(5):433-440.

Wilson RS, Krueger KR. Loneliness and risk of Alzheimer's disease. Archives of General Psychiatry 2007 Feb;64(2)34-40.

Scarmeas N, Levy G et al. Influence of leisure activity on the incidence of Alzheimer's disease. Neurology 2001;57:2236-2242.

Buckwalter KC, Gerdner LA. Shining through: the humor and individuality of persons with Alzheimer's disease. Journal of Gerontological Nursing 1995 Mar;21(3):11-6.

Dhikay V, Anand KS. Glucocorticoids may initiate Alzheimer's disease: a potential therapeutic role for mifepriostone (RU-486). Medical Hypotheses 2006 Nov 13;68(5):1088-92.

Wilson RS, Arnold SE et al. Chronic distress, age-related neuropathology and late-life dementia. Psychosomatic Medicine 2007 Jan-Feb;69(1):47-53.

Elias MF, Sullivan LM. Left ventricular mass, blood pressure, and lowered cognitive performance in the Framingham offspring. Hypertension 2007 Mar;49(3):439-45.

Comiis HC, Dik MG. Predictors of dementia, the construction of classification trees. Tijdschrift voor gerontologie en geriatrie 2006 Dec;37(6):237-42.

Van den Berg E, Kessels RP. Type 2 diabetes, cognitive function and dementia: vascular and metabolic determinants. Drugs Today 2006 Nov;42(11):741-54.

Isoniemi H, Tenuwuo O. Outcome of traumatic brain injury after three decades—relationship to ApoE genotype. Journal of Neurotrauma 2006 Nov;23(11):1600-8.

Phung TK, Andersen K. Lifestyle-related risk factors for dementia. Ugeskrift for laeger 2006 Oct 2;168(40):3401-5.

Gatz M, Prescott CA. Lifestyle risk and delaying factors. Alzheimer's Disease and Associated Disorders 2006 Jul-Sep;200(3 Supl 2):584-8.

Ermini-Funfschilling D, Stahelin HB. Is prevention of dementia possible? Zeitschrift fur Gerontologie 1993 Nov-Dec;26(6):446-52.

Young SF, Mainoux AG 3rd et al. Hyperinsulinemia and cognitive decline in a middle-aged cohort. Diabetes Care 2006 Dec;29(12): 2688-93.

Dziedzic T. Systemic inflammatory markers and risk of dementia. American Journal of Alzheimer's Disease and Other Dementias 2006 Aug-Sep;21(4):258-62.

Ances BM, Ellis RJ. Dementia and neurocognitive disorders due to HIV-1 infection. Seminars in Neurology 2007 Feb;27(1):86-92.

Scarmeas N, Stern Y. Mediterranean diet, Alzheimer disease and vascular mediation. Archives of Neurology 2006 Dec;63(12);1709-17.

Jarvenpaa T, Rinne JO. Binge drinking in midlife and dementia risk. Epidemiology 2005 Nov;16(6):766-71.

Skotko BG, Kensinger EA. Puzzling thoughts for H.M.: can new semantic information be anchored to old semantic memories? Neuropsychology 2004 Oct;18(4):756-69.

Ho YC, Cheung MC et al. Music training improves verbal but not visual memory: cross-sectional and longitudinal explorations in children. Neuropsychology 2003 Jul;17(3):439-50.

Verghese J, Lipton RB. Leisure activities and the risk of dementia in the elderly. New England journal of Medicine 2003 Jun 19;348(25):2489-90.

Convit A, Wolf OT. Reduced glucose tolerance is associated with poor memory performance and hippocampal atrophy among normal elderly. Proceedings of the National Academy of Sciences of the USA 2003 Feb 18;100(4);2019-22.

Morris MC, Evans DA et al. Consumption of fish and N-3 fatty acids and the risk of Alzheimer disease. Archives of Neurology 2003 Jul;60(7):940-6.

Wang JY, Zhou DH. Leisure activity and risk of cognitive impairment: the Chongqing aging study. Neurology 2006 Mar 28'66(8):911-3.

Fogel J, Carlsoon MC. Soap operas and talk shows on television are associated with poorer cognition in older women. The Southern Medical Journal 2006 Mar;99(3):226-33.

Tarraga L, Boada M et al. A randomized pilot study to assess the efficacy of an interactive multimedia tool of cognitive stimulation in Alzheimer's disease. Journal of Neurology, Neuropsychiatry and Psychiatry 2006 Oct;77(10):-1116-21.

Keller KB, Lemberg L. Retirement is no excuse for physical inactivity or isolation. American Journal of Critical Care 2002 May;11(3):270-2.

Simonsick EM, Lafferty ME et al. Risk due to inactivity in physically capable older adults. American Journal of Public Health 1993;10(83):1443-1450.

Doll, Peto R et al. Smoking and dementia in male British doctors. British Medical Journal 2000 Apr 22;320(7242):1097- 102.

Bourre JM. Effects of nutrients (in food) on the structure and function of the nervous system; update on dietary requirements for brain. Part 2: macronutrients. Journal of Nutrition. Health and Aging 2006 Sep-Oct;10(5):386-99.

Andersen K, Lolk A et al. Depression and the risk of Alzheimer's disease. Ugeskrift for laeger 2006 Oct 2;168(40):3409-12.

Small GW, Silverman DH. Effects of a 14-day healthy longevity lifestyle program on cognition and brain function. American Journal of Geriatrics and Psychiatry 2006 Jun;14(6):5 38-45.

Drummond SP, Brown GG et al. Sleep deprivation-induced reduction in cortical functional response to serial subtraction. NeuroReport 1999;10(18):3745-3748.

Drummond SP, Brown GG et al. Altered brain response to verbal learning following sleep deprivation. Nature 2000;403(6770):655-7.

Drummond SP, Gillin JC et al. Increased cerebral response during a divided attention task following sleep deprivation. Journal of Sleep Research 2001;10(2):85-92.

Fenn KM, Nusbaum, HC et al. Consolidation during sleep of perceptual learning of spoken language. Nature 2003;425: 614-616.

Frank MG, Issa NP et al. Sleep Enhances Plasticity in the Developing Visual Cortex. Neuron 2005;30:275-287.

Ohayon, MM, Vecchierini MF. Daytime sleepiness and cognitive impairment in the elderly population. Archives of Internal Medicine 2002:162: 201-8.

Walker MP, Brakefield T et al. Dissociable stages of human memory consolidation and reconsolidation. Nature 2003;425:616-620.

Watson GS, Craft S. Modulation of memory by insulin and glucose: neuropsychological observations in Alzheimer's disease. European Journal of Pharmacology 2004 Apr 19;490(1-3):971-13.

Bialystok, E., et al. Bilingualism as a protection against the onset of symptoms of dementia. Neuropsychologia 2007;45:459-464.

Improve Your Learning Skills

Thus far, I've focused largely on what you as an individual can do to preserve your mental function as you age.

Now I'd like to talk about expanding your mental function, increasing your learning capacity, and best of all, helping younger people maximize their brain function. I've made this a separate chapter to underscore its importance to you and your children and grandchildren.

THE SAD IS SAD FOR SCHOOL PERFORMANCE

Let me discuss SAD (the standard American diet). So many young people today eat such nutrient-poor diets that they cannot possibly have the brain function they need to learn the basics for survival in the modern world. Did you ever wonder why Johnny can't read or Sara can't do simple multiplication tables?

Maybe the fault lies with poor nutrition rather than with failing schools or poorly paid teachers or bad study habits or busy parents.

Kids who are subsisting on pop tarts, Doritos, Happy Meals, and gulping down gallons of Coke are at risk of many problems including a dramatically reduced ability to take in and remember new information.

We know that children who have diets high in processed foods and simple sugars are also at risk for behavioral problems.

Now we know that kids who eat a healthy diet improve their academic performance as well as increasing their ability to fit into the mainstream at school.

In a study done in 803 New York public schools and in nine juvenile correction facilities, researchers found that increased amounts of fruits, vegetables and whole grains and decreased fat and sugars made some dramatic changes.

After two years of improved diet with no other changes in their lifestyles, the academic performance of 1.1 million children rose 16% and learning disabilities fell 40%.

In the juvenile correction facilities, violent and non-violent antisocial behavior fell 48%.

According to one of the researchers, the schools have not instituted any of these dietary changes on a permanent basis. Instead, the school systems and the medical profession prefer to keep children with learning and behavior disabilities on prescription drugs. Parents who have refused to drug their children may be turned in to authorities for medical negligence. Yet, these are the same schools that promote poor dietary habits by embracing candy and soda machines on their campuses on the premise that sales from these machines raise needed funds for the school—at the expense of our children's learning abilities!

These impressive figures drive home the point that a child's ability to grow and succeed in the world can be greatly improved by a healthy diet.

A MULTI FOR EVERY KID

In 2002, the *Journal of the American Medical Association* reversed its long-standing distaste for vitamin supplements and recommended multi-vitamins for every adult.

This is a step in the right direction, but so far, the AMA has not endorsed the idea of a multi-vitamin for every child.

That's too bad, since this simple type of supplementation appears to go a long way toward improving school performance and learning ability.

One study sponsored by the University of California and conducted on poorly nourished school children and young men in American correctional facilities in four U.S. states as well as England, Wales, Scotland and Belgium who received supplements performed better on standard IQ tests by 3.2 points than those who did not receive supplements.

Another impressive study showed that kids in two working class elementary schools in Phoenix who were given supplements that supplied just half of the U.S. recommended Daily Allowance (RDA) were able to improve their results on IQ tests, some of them by as much as 15 points!

These two studies were done on children with poor dietary habits. Their importance is underscored by the fact that, in both studies, children who were already consuming healthy diets did not improve on the intelligence tests.

We also know that pregnant women who eat fish or take fish oil supplements produce smarter babies and their children are better able to learn in the first five years of life.

A growing body of research is also showing us that proper levels of B vitamins (especially B12 and folate), iron, vitamins C, D and K are vital to the ability to learn at any age.

IMPROVING IQ

Technically, it's not possible to improve the intelligence you were born with, but it is possible to improve your score on IQ tests by a number of methods that quite literally train your brain.

IQ tests measure a few human abilities, including short-term memory, verbal knowledge, spatial visualization, logic and reasoning.

IQ tests do not measure many important areas of life, including creative, musical and leadership skills. However, they are generally considered reliable indicators of future success and job performance.

Performance on IQ tests is as subjective as it can be on any type of test and can be affected by a number of factors, including your physical state of health at the time of the test, the amount of sleep you've had, the environment in which you took the test, stress levels, etc.

TYPES OF IQ TESTING AND SCORING

There are two basic types of IQ tests: those given to children and those given to adults.

Those given to children (the most common is Stanford-Binet Intelligence Scale) are scored by dividing the test taker's mental age by her chronological age and multiplying by 100. For example, a 10-year old who scored at the level of a 13-year old would be scored as follows:

100X Mental age (13)
Chronological age (10) = IQ (130)

A later version of IQ testing, called the Wechsler scale, was developed for adults and bases its scores on population distribution rather than on age.

A score of 100 on a Wechsler IQ test would put you squarely in the average category since 50% of those taking the test scored lower than you did and 50% scored higher.

- An IQ of 110 is higher than 75% of all persons taking the test.
- An IQ of 120 is higher than 93% of all persons taking the test.
- An IQ of 130 is higher than 98% of all persons taking the test.

IQ scores are typically not divulged to children and only rarely reported to their families because of the potential stigma and damage to self-esteem it could cause them, particularly for those who have subnormal scores.

In general, our IQs do not change in our lifetimes, but certainly as you learned in Chapter 5, your mental capabilities can be honed and trained and sharpened, which will serve you well throughout your life. All of the recommendations for memory improvement in Chapter 5 also apply to improving IQ.

**You may not be able to literally become more
intelligent, but you certainly can improve your ability
to learn, your ability to function on tests and to raise
your scores on IQ tests.**

I'll remind you here: You cannot really improve your intelligence, but you can improve your score on your IQ tests, and that is a worthwhile endeavor for maintaining brain function.

So the first step, if you want to improve your IQ, is to take an IQ test so you can establish a baseline.

TRAIN YOUR BRAIN

There hasn't been much scientific research done on these methods, but they certainly make sense and it would do you no harm to try them.

Here are a few common recommendations:

Expand your vocabulary: Daily vocabulary drills are basically a memorization skill. You can work your way through the dictionary or sign up for an e-mail word-a-day challenge at www.dictionary.com. Even Reader's Digest has an interesting vocabulary quiz every month. You can also expand your vocabulary by reading extensively, talking to people, and by playing board games like Scrabble.

Improve your test-taking skills: IQ tests are almost always multiple choice. Many test-taking techniques will help you to work quickly and accurately. Use your logical mind and eliminate impossible choices and find standout choices. There are many techniques to help you at any of a wide vareity of websites you can find by Googling test-taking strategies.

Learn how to use an abacus: Researchers in India found that children who were trained to use an abacus improved their short-term memory skills. The scientists theorized that the use of the abacus required extensive right- and left-brain communication.

Meditate: Several studies have shown that children and adults who meditate can improve their IQ scores. There are no scientific explanations for the phenomenon, but my guess is that meditation does not actually increase intelligence. Instead, I think it probably helps the test taker be more focused and relaxed, resulting in higher scores.

Fake it till you make it: If you believe you are smarter, you actually become smarter. Many of us sabotage our own success through self-sabotage. Make a note of your successes. Start telling yourself, "Hey, that was really creative," when you do something creative. When you have a good idea, make a note of it. Gather the evidence for your own IQ improvement and you'll start to experience more of it as you believe in it.

Play Mozart: This phenomenon has become so widely studied it has a name: The Mozart Effect. In one study, 36 students were given three spatial reasoning tests on a standard IQ test. Just before the first test, they listened to Mozart's Sonata for Two Pianos in D Major, K. 448 for ten minutes. Before the second test, they listened to a relaxation tape. Before the third, they sat in silence. The average scores for all 36 students: 1st test: 119. 2nd test: 111. 3rd test: 110. Mozart helped improved test scores by nine points!

While there are those who would argue with the validity of the Mozart Effect, there is no doubt that it at least induces relaxation and probably does something even more to enhance brain function because of the music's highly organized structure.

One study from the University of California, showed children who studied a musical instrument were much better at solving puzzles and scored 80% higher on spatial intelligence tests than a non-musical group.

Several studies show that people who studied piano and sang daily also perform better on memory tests.

Switch it around. Keep challenging yourself to higher levels of achievement. For example, if you play the piano, try playing without looking at the keys. When that becomes easy, try playing without looking at the sheet music. I'm sure you can find many ways to apply this idea to any activity you enjoy.

IN CONCLUSION

In addition to my 30-Day Jump-Start Your Brain Program in Chapter 5, there are many techniques that will improve your concentration and levels for alertness. These will most likely increase your scores on IQ tests. Since few of us brag about our IQs, there is little value for this except the personal satisfaction of knowing you are doing everything you can to keep your brain healthy, engaged and active.

References:

Schoenthaler SJ, Bier ID. Vitamin-mineral intake and intelligence: a macrolevel analysis of randomized controlled trials. Journal of Alternative and Complementary Medicine 1999 Apr;5(2):125-34.

Schoenthaler SJ, Bier ID et al. The effect of vitamin-mineral supplementation on the intelligence of American schoolchildren: a randomized, double-blind placebo-controlled trial. Journal of Alternative and Complementary Medicine 2000 Feb;6(1):19-29.

Helland IB, Smith L et al. Maternal supplementation with very-long-chain n-3 fatty acids during pregnancy and lactation augments children's IQ at 4 years of age. Pediatrics 2003 Jan;111(1):39-44.

Hibbeln JR, Davis JM. Maternal seafood consumption in pregnancy and neurodevelopmental outcomes in childhood (ALSPAC study): an observational cohort study. Lancet 2007 Feb 17;369(9561):578-8.

Boure JM. Effects of nutrients (in food) on the structure and function of the nervous system: update on dietary requirements for brain. Part 1: micronutrients. Journal of Nutrition, Health and Aging 2006 Sep-Oct;10(5):377-85.

Whalley LJ, Fox JC. Cognitive aging, childhood intelligence, and the use of food supplements: possible involvement of n-3 fatty acids. American Journal of Clinical Nutrition 2004 Dec;80(6):1650-7.

Bhaskaran M, Sengottaiyan A. Evaluation of memory in abacus learners. Indian Journal of Physiological Pharmacology 2006 Jul-Sep; 50(3):225-33.

Rosaen C, Benn R. The experience of transcendental meditation in middle school students: a qualitative report. Explore (NY) 2006 Sep-Oct;2(5):422-5.

Jedrczak A, Toomey M. The TM-Sidhi programme, age and brief tests of perceptual-motor speed and nonverbal intelligence. Journal of Clinical Psychology 1986 Jan;42(1):161-4.

Hughes JS. The Mozart Effect. Epilepsy and Behavior 2001 Oct;2(5):386-417.

Twomey A, Esgate A. The Mozart Effect may only be demonstrable in nonmusicians. Perceptual and Motor Skills 2002 Dec;95(3 Pt 1);1013-26.

Kennedy DO, Scholey AB. The psychopharmacology of European herbs with cognition-enhancing properties. Current Pharmaceutical Design 2006;12(35):4613-23.

Eat for Long Memory and Long Life

Here's some more good news: If you're already eating a healthy diet, you're probably already doing the best you can to preserve your memory.

What's a good diet?

The vast majority of Americans don't know the answer to that question.

Americans consume on average, just under three servings of fruits and vegetables a day. That's if you include the ketchup we slather on trans-fatty-acid-soaked French fries.

That's appalling! For decades, the government has encouraged us to eat five servings of fruits and vegetables a day. The vigorous campaign hasn't budged us off our national addiction to meat and potatoes, cakes and pies, corn chips, potato chips, Twinkies and other junk food.

If you eat that way, you don't know how to eat and your life will be shortened. I can't say it any more clearly than that. Poor dietary habits are the primary cause of heart disease, diabetes and cancer that are shortening our lives.

I'm not suggesting you go on a tofu and sprout diet or any such thing. All you need to do is to eat rationally.

I'm not going to give you an entire textbook on nutrition, but there are some basics everyone needs to know for general overall health. I promise, I'll make it painless.

All food falls into three categories: proteins, fats and carbohydrates. They are essential to human life.

- **Proteins** include all types of meat, fish, dairy products, legumes (dried beans and peas) and nuts.
- **Carbohydrates** are all sorts of fruits, vegetables, grains, sugars and all products made from them.
- **Fats** come in several forms. The most important for you to know right now are saturated fats that come from animals and polyunsaturated fats that come from fish, seeds and nuts.

If you eat your food as close to its natural state as possible, you'll be doing yourself a great nutritional favor.

Processed foods are not only nutritionally null, they contain additives, preservatives, trans fatty acids and all sorts of other nastiness that is detrimental to your health.

I once heard a great piece of advice on how to shop: Shop the perimeter of your supermarket. For the most part, that is where the fresh and whole foods are.

Here's the key: Emphasize the beans and nuts for your protein needs; fruits, vegetables and whole grains for your carbs; and nut and seed oils for your fats. It's as simple as that.

In addition to eating for general well-being, there are particular types of foods that specifically contribute to brain health and memory preservation.

Here is the best of the best:

Eat fish: Fish is an important part of any healthy diet, and it is the Number One food to help promote brain health. Fish has long been known as "brain food" because it helps preserve memory, elevates mood and generally keeps cognitive function on track. In fact, numerous studies support the idea that Omega-3 fatty acids unique to fatty, coldwater fish can ease depression, improve attention span, sharpen mental function and improve memory.

Since more than 60 percent of the human brain is composed of fat, one-third of it Omega-3 fatty acids, it stands to reason that improving Omega-3 intake would have a positive effect on mental function and mood and the reverse would be true when there are shortfalls in Omega-3s in our diets and supplements.

Omega-3s are also believed to help improve blood flow to the brain through their effects on the cardiovascular system.

Omega-3s are also linked to levels of the brain chemical phosphatidylserine (PS) which promotes healthy memory and emotional state with aging. (Learn more about PS in Chapter 8.)

Regular fish intake—as little as one serving a week—can reduce the risk of Alzheimer's disease by 60 percent, says a dramatic study from Chicago's Rush Institute for Healthy Aging.

The Chicago researchers say Omega-3 component DHA (docosahexaenoic acid) is most likely the ingredient that protects the brain from beta amyloid plaque and tangles of nerves believed to be a major factor in Alzheimer's.

Salmon, tuna, sardines and mackerel are the best sources of Omega-3s, and I recommend you get three servings of wild-caught, coldwater fish every week. Farm-raised fish have a lower Omega-3 content because they are fed on a grain diet. Farm-raised fish also carry a high toxic load because of the pesticides and the growth enhancers used in the farming operations. They may also contain high levels of mercury.

Those healthy fats are important at the earliest stages of life. A study recently published in the British medical journal, *The Lancet*, found that women who ate no seafood at all during pregnancy had babies in the lowest 48 percent of the intelligence scale, while those who ate a modest amount of seafood (about 11 ounces a week) had the smartest babies, suggesting that government recommendations for pregnant women to limit their seafood intake may actually be harmful to the intelligence of children. Instead, I'd recommend the healthiest seafood possible and Omega-3 supplements for everyone, particularly pregnant women.

Not a fan of fish? Are you allergic to fish? Not a problem! You can do just as well without any mercury risk by taking a good quality Omega-3 supplement made from molecularly distilled fish oil. I recommend taking at least 1,200 to 2,400 mg a day. Look for a brand that includes 800 mg of EPA and 400 mg of DHA, the two most important nutrients in these healthy oils.

A recent study from Tufts University showed that older people who had the highest DHA in their bloodstreams were 39 percent less likely to get Alzheimer's and a 47 percent lower risk of other types of dementia.

This should convince you. I'm convinced that fish and fish oil supplements are essential to helping preserve memory and overall health.

Eat healthy fats: Good fats should be a part of everyone's diet.

The American people developed a phobia about fat during the low-fat diet craze a decade or so ago. Actually, we all need fat for heart health and a wider variety of bodily functions. Where most of Americans get into trouble is by eating the wrong types of fats. The standard American diet (SAD) is heavy in saturated animal fats from meat, butter, cheese and other animal fats and very low in the healthy polyunsaturated fats. We want to reverse that ratio and get most of our fats from nuts and seeds.

Olive oil is one of the best known fats—and one of the healthiest. There is lots of scientific evidence that shows monounsaturated fats such as olive oil also help preserve memory. Olive oil is a good choice for low temperature cooking as well for salad dressings. Organic extra virgin olive oil, the best quality, is my favorite healthy oil. Canola, walnut and flaxseed oils are also good healthy oils.

Nuts of virtually all kinds are excellent sources of healthy fats, protein and other essential nutrients.

A good rule of thumb is that if a fat is solid at room temperature (with the exception of coconut oil) it's probably not good for you.

Eat good carbs: Carbohydrates provide fuel for the brain. Without them, brain function becomes sluggish. The Institute of Medicine says we need 130 grams of carbohydrates daily for maximum brain function. This may explain why people on the extreme low-carb diets like the Atkins diet (allowing only 20 grams of carbs per day) complain of brain fog.

To get the optimal amount, you need several servings of high-quality carbohydrates a day. By good carbs, I'm not talking about cakes and pies or even those so-called healthy energy bars that are often loaded with sugar. I means fruits and vegetables (see the next sections) and a modest amount of whole grains.

Here are some examples of healthy carbohydrate choices that will give you pretty much what you need for a day: a cup of organic steel-cut oatmeal, 25 grams; a large apple, 29 grams; a cup of brown rice, 44 grams; and a sweet potato, 23 grams.

Avoid processed sugars and table sugar at all costs. Any simple carbohydrates can give you that sluggish feeling that makes it difficult to think. This is because your pancreas is dumping insulin into your system, which can result in blood sugar fluctuations. Don't eat white flour, sugar, soft drinks, pastries, cookies, etc. You get the idea.

Eat a minimum of five servings of fresh fruits and vegetables daily: I work at getting nine a day, because they are all low in calories and packed with nutritional value.

And they can literally add years to your life. Research correlates longevity to fruit and vegetable consumption, which means the more fruits and veggies you eat, the longer you're likely to live. As just one example, a recent study reported that rats fed a blueberry-supplemented diet had enhanced behavioral performance and significantly less brain cell loss.

Fruits and vegetables should be the foundation of your eating program. Eat them first and add other foods in more sparing amounts. Eat some of them raw and lightly steam others. Fresh is best, but frozen fruits and vegetables are acceptable. Canned fruits are loaded with sugar and canned vegetables (except tomato products and beans) are almost completely devoid of nutrients. Microwaving also destroys most of the nutrients in fruits and vegetables.

I recommend eating organic produce as much as possible because it is simply healthier, it's good for the environment and it helps reduce the toxic load most of us carry from pesticides and other toxins we're exposed to in our everyday lives that may contribute to memory problems later in life.

Here are the top five fruits and vegetables in terms of nutritional value:

- Broccoli and other cruciferous vegetables, including cauliflower and cabbage
- All types of berries, especially blueberries, blackberries, strawberries, raspberries and cranberries
- Apples
- Spinach and other dark green leafy vegetables
- Cooked tomatoes

Eat a wide variety of these health powerhouses as well as all other types of fruits and veggies to get the strongest possible protection against the common diseases of aging.

Moderate alcohol consumption: A few years ago, it would have been unthinkable to suggest that drinking alcoholic beverages would be part of a healthy diet, but here we are in the 21st century and we've learned that moderate alcohol consumption is not only acceptable, it's in your best interests.

I would never suggest that you start drinking just for the health benefits, but if you already enjoy a glass or two of red wine daily, I'd encourage you to keep it up. It will do wonders for your health.

It will most likely protect your brain and preserve your memory. Danish researchers found that moderate consumption of wine significantly reduced the risk of dementia in healthy elderly subjects, while other types of alcohol and beer did not have the protective effect. Not only is wine protective of brain tissue and memory function, its heart-healthy and cancer-protective benefits have been scientifically validated and documented.

It is often touted as a longevity booster, for good reason. Red wine contains two of the most powerful antioxidants known to science, resveratrol and oligomeric procyanadins.

So what is moderate consumption? It's simple: a glass of wine a day for women and two glasses for men. Much more than that and you flip very quickly into increasing your risk of various health problems, including breast cancer for women.

Drink coffee and tea: This is another one of those, "Oh no, I thought these were bad for me" recommendations.

Science is increasingly telling us that caffeine intake, in moderate amounts, is good for us in several ways, including protecting our brains from the destructive elements of dementia. One sizeable European study says that non-coffee drinkers have more than four times the risk of Alzheimer's as those who love their java.

Tea of all types has somewhat less caffeine than coffee, but can offer protective effects as well.

You may be a green tea drinker and that's great. This minimally processed form of tea contains a wealth of health benefits, including protection from memory loss. Researchers credit a unique flavonoid compound called epigallocatechin-3-gallate (EGCG) with helping to stop the formation of the beta amyloid plaques characteristic of Alzheimer's. I'll tell you more about that in Chapter 8.

All types of teas and coffee contain caffeine. There is even a small amount in the decaffeinated varieties.

Caffeine appears to work in your favor to preserve brain cells in

three ways, according to the British Alzheimer's Society:
- It stimulates brain cells to take in choline, the building block needed to make acetylcholine, a brain chemical that is reduced in people with dementia.
- It interferes with another brain chemical called adenosine that may knock out other brain chemicals and open pathways for Alzheimer's.
- It may slow down the sometimes frantic activity of glia cells, the housekeepers of the brain that keep it clean. At times, their activity can sometimes be too thorough, and can damage surrounding brain areas.

Too much coffee, however, can have many adverse health effects; so it's best to limit your intake to three cups a day or less.

IN CONCLUSION

Eat well and eat the right foods. Your body will reward you with a long, healthy life and your brain will be capable of clear thinking well into old age.

References:

Morris MC, Evans DA et al. Consumption of fish and n-3 fatty acids and risk of incident Alzheimer disease. Archives of Neurology 2003 Jul;60(7):923-4.

Hibbeln JR et al. Beneficial effects of Maternal seafood intake on neurodevelopmental outcomes in their children. Lancet 2007;369:578-585.

Bourre JM. Dietary omega-3 fatty acids for women. Biomedicine and Pharmacology 2007 Feb-Apr;61(2-3):105-12.

Schaefer EJ. Bongard V et al. High plasma phosphatidylcholine DHA content associated with reduced risk of dementia. Archives of Neurology 2006;63(11):1545-50.

Kotani S, Sakaguchi E et al. Supplementation with arachidonic acid and docosahexaenoic acid may improve cognitive dysfunction. Neuroscience Research 2006 Oct;56(2):159-64.

Perez-Jimenez F, Alvarez de Cienfuegos G et al. International conference on the healthy effect of virgin olive oil. European Journal of Clinical Investigations 2005 Jul;35(7):421-4.

Morris MC, Evans DA et al. Association of vegetable and fruit consumption with age-related cognitive change. Neurology 2006 Oct 24;67(8):1370-6.

Treulsen T, Thudium D et al. Amount and type of alcohol and risk of dementia: the Copenhagen City Heart Study. Neurology 2002 Nov 12;59(9):1300-1.

Valenzano DR, Cellerino A. Resveratrol and the pharmacology of aging: a new vertebrate model to validate an old model. Cell Cycle 2006 May;5(10):1027-32.

Koo SH, Montminy M. In vino veritas: a tale of two sirt1s? Cell 2006 Dec 15;127(6):1091-3.

Gronbaek M, Deis A et al. Mortality associated with moderate intakes of wine, beer or spirits. British Medical Journal 1995 May 310(6988):1165-9.

van Gelder B. Coffee consumption is inversely associated with cognitive decline in elderly European men: the FINE study. European Journal of Clinical Nutrition 2007;61:226-232.

Arendash GW, Schlief W et al. Caffeine protects Alzheimer's mice against cognitive impairment and reduces brain beat-amyloid production. Neuroscience 2006 Nov 3;142(4):941-52.

Rezal-Zadeh K, Shytle D et al. Green tea epigallocatechin-3-gallate (EGCG) modulates amyloid precursor protein cleavage and reduces cerebral amyloidosis in Alzheimer transgenic mice. Journal of Neuroscience 2005 Sep 21;25(38):8807-14.

Duffy KB et al. A blueberry-enriched diet provides cellular protection against oxidative stress and reduces a kainate-induced learning impairment in rats. Neurobiology Aging 2007 May 22 (Epub ahead of print).

The Right Supplements

Supplements are an important element of keeping your brain healthy, your mental function intact and, of course, preserving your memory.

In this chapter, I'll recommend a few really essential supplements that I think everyone should take and others to consider if you are at especially high risk or you have other reasons for taking them.

I am not a fan of indiscriminate taking of supplements and I certainly don't recommend routinely taking dozens of pills a day.

I know there is an element of faith in taking supplements, because you never can be absolutely sure what they have prevented. There really isn't any answer to the legitimate doubts that you may be wasting your money or taking things you don't need. The only thing I can say to put your doubts to rest is that the human body is a machine and we are beginning to understand it better and better every day. We know that it cannot function without a basic set of nutrients. If or when things do start to go wrong, we have to rely on research to help correct the shortfalls to get that machine back to its peak performance.

Please remember that less is always better.

Everyone is unique, so you'll need to experiment at the lower dosages and move higher (to the maximum recommended dosage) only after you're certain the lower dosage is not effective.

Also remember that many of these nutrients are slow acting. Most of them don't work like taking an aspirin for a headache and it's gone in 20 minutes. While some may have fairly quick responses, give a nutrient a fair try. Unless you're having some side effects, use it for at least eight weeks, and better yet, try it for 12 weeks before you decide it isn't for you.

Finally, these supplements have no serious side effects or interactions with prescription drugs unless otherwise noted. However, it is always wise to check with your doctor before taking these or any other supplements.

THE ESSENTIALS

Here's the short list:

A good multi-vitamin

Even the staid American Medical Association has finally agreed that all adults need a multi-vitamin every day because of shortfalls in our diets and deteriorating soil conditions that make it virtually impossible to get all the nutrients we need for optimum health. Even if you eat the best possible diet, you still need a multi-vitamin. Here's my recommendation:

Beta-tene (natural carotenoids)	5,000-25,000 IU
Vitamin B1 (thiamine)	50-200 mg
Vitamin B2 (riboflavin)	10-20 mg
Vitamin B3 (niacinamide)	100-200 mg
Vitamin B5 (pantothenic acid)	10-200 mg
Vitamin B6 (pyridoxine)	50-200 mg
Vitamin B12 (methylcobalamin)	500 mcg-5 mg
Folic acid	800 mcg-5 mg
Biotin	500 mcg-5 mg
Vitamin C	500-2,000 mg
Vitamin D	400-4,000 IU
Vitamin E (D-alpha succinate)	100-800 IU
Calcium (citrate malate)	500-1,300 mg
Magnesium	250-500 mg
Zinc (L-OptiZinc®)	15-30 mg
Copper	1-2 mg
Manganese	1-2 mg
Boron	1-3 mg
Selenium (selenomethionine)	200-400 mcg
Chromium	200-500 mcg
Lutein	6-20 mg
Bioflavonoids (quercetin is best)	100-500 mg
Acetyl L-carnitine	500-2,000 mg
Alpha lipoic acid	150-1200 mg
Grapeseed and green tea antioxidants	50-1,000 mg
Coenzyme Q10	100-1,200 mg

The ranges included here are based on published studies showing their benefits in human supplementation. Most of these levels cannot be obtained through diet alone. The lower ranges can be obtained through about two capsules a day. To get dosages in the higher ranges, you'll need to take six to eight capsules a day or more.

You may not find a single product that contains these precise amounts. Check your multi-vitamin label carefully to see what's included and add whatever is missing. The cheap "A-to-Z, all-purpose, one-a-day" vitamin tablets aren't going to come close to what you need.

Most multi-vitamins are horribly inadequate to meet your nutritional needs. In fact, the most popular brand only costs the manufacturer about two cents per tablet to produce. What can you buy that is worth having that costs two cents? The answer is NOTHING! I strongly recommend that you spend enough to get real protection and real benefits. The cost should be between $1 and $2 a day for good health.

This is the foundation of your supplement plan. All adults need these nutrients.

Antioxidants

Think of your body as a car. Over time, your car gets a few dings and scrapes, a little rust on the bumper and some sludge in the engine. If you don't take care of those problems, eventually the body rusts through and the engine seizes up and it stops running. Off to the car graveyard.

Your body works in much the same way. Through the process of daily living and the passage of time, our cells start to throw off these disease-causing molecules called free radicals. They act just like rust in your cells, messing up your entire body system, damaging DNA so the cells can no longer repair themselves or accurately reproduce themselves and eventually causing the diseases of aging from heart disease to cancer, diabetes, stroke and dementia.

You've probably heard of antioxidants. To make it simple, these substances act like scrub brushes, neutralizing those free radical molecules, reducing the inflammation they cause and sweeping them out of the body.

The best known antioxidants are vitamins A, C and E. I add B vitamins to this list, especially B12, because they have some unique antioxidant functions for brain health. These substances are extremely important to your basic health plan and you should get loads of them in a fruit- and vegetable-laden diet and in supplements as recommended in your daily multi-vitamins. However, there are other nutrients that are hundreds and perhaps thousands of times more powerful. Among them are:
- Omega-3 fatty acids (as in fish oil)
- Acetyl L-carnitine
- Alpha lipoic acid
- Resveratrol
- Green tea extract
- Aged garlic extract

Consider adding some or all of them to your supplementation plan, since each one has unique properties and special benefits.

Here are the antioxidants I think are best for keeping your memory and slowing down cognitive decline if it has begun:

Omega-3 fatty acids

Every single cell in your body needs good fats in the form of Omega-3 fatty acids. They're also called essential fatty acids for a reason: They are essential to all aspects of human health and are particularly important for optimal heart function, joint health, maternal and child health and, of course, brain health.

Omega-3 fatty acids should be part of everyone's diet. They're found in abundance in fatty, coldwater fish such as salmon, tuna, mackerel and anchovies. They're also found to a much smaller degree in flaxseed, nuts, nut oils, canola oil and green leafy vegetables. Vegetable sources of Omega-3s are not easily converted for your body's use, so you need more, lots more—maybe three times as much.

I'd go so far as to say that, if I could take only one supplement, it would most likely be the highest quality fish oil I could find.

Numerous studies support the idea that Omega-3s from fatty, coldwater fish can ease depression, improve attention span, sharpen mental function and improve memory.

The most important study on people with varying degrees of memory loss and Omega-3s came from Sweden in late 2006. It showed, as we might expect, that Omega-3s did not have any benefit for those with advanced memory loss because their brain cells were already lost. However, for those with very mild memory loss, there was a significant slowing in memory decline for those who took the Omega-3s, possibly because of their anti-inflammatory effects.

The famous Framingham Heart study also found that elderly people were 47% less likely to have failing memories if they had high levels of DHA (docosahexaenoic acid), a major component of fish oil, in their bloodstreams.

Unfortunately, because so much fish on the market today is contaminated with mercury and other heavy metals, the government warns that we shouldn't eat more than two servings of fish a week.

Most of us don't get anywhere enough Omega-3s; most of us get far too many Omega-6s. These are also essential fatty acids, crucial to human health in small amounts, but present in the standard american diet (SAD) in large amounts. Omega-6s are found in vegetable oils like those used for cooking: sunflower, corn, safflower, soybean and all those oils that drench our French fries in unhealthy fats that seem to be a staple of the SAD.

Experts say the best possible ratio of Omega-6s to Omega-3s should be 1:1, but even 2:1 or 3:1 wouldn't be too bad. Sadly, the average American gets 20:1 or even 50:1, setting us up for health problems.

Let's put it in the simplest possible way: The more Omega-3s you get, the healthier you will be. It sounds like Omega 3s can do anything. Is it the snake oil of the 21st century?

Not at all.

There have been literally many hundreds of studies over the past 25 years affirming the benefits of Omega-3 fatty acids, not only for brain protection, but for heart health, joint health, cancer protection and even protection for pregnant women and their infants, to give those developing brains the best possible start.

The Omega-3s in coldwater, fatty fish are the best source of these essential fats. But what's in the fish oil? Two major elements are responsible for the health benefits:

- **DHA** (docosahexaenoic acid) has many positive effects, but perhaps the most impressive is its ability to help lower triglycerides. High triglycerides have been linked to heart disease. Research also shows that DHA is important for helping pregnant women carry their babies to full term and give them the maximum nourishment through breast milk, for visual and neurological development in infants, learning in young children, normalizing brain function, emotional and psychological well-being, preserving eyesight, insulin resistance (pre-diabetes and diabetes) and easing digestive and reproductive difficulties.
- **EPA** (eicosapentanoic acid) is credited with helping to reduce excessive blood clotting that can lead to heart disease. EPA also plays a role in reducing stress, keeping physical energy levels up, eye health and good brain function.

How can you best get those all-important Omega-3s into your diet? The best way is to get a high-quality Omega-3 fatty acid supplement.

Dosage: Take 1,200 mg to 2,400 mg of EPA and DHA every day.

How can you determine the quality of your fish oil? Look for a molecularly distilled and concentrated fish oil to eliminate any toxins in the fish used for the oil.

B vitamins

The eight unique nutrients in the B-vitamin group include B1 (thiamine), B2 (riboflavin), B3 (niacin or niacinamide), B5 (pantothenic acid), B6 (pyridoxine), biotin, B12 (methylcobalamin in its most active form), folate or folic acid and choline.

B vitamins are essential to energy production and proper nerve function and play a vital role in brain health. You can usually find all of the recommended dosages in one simple B-complex capsule.

Individual B vitamins have additional functions:

- Thiamine is essential to proper cognitive function, heart function and maintenance of muscle mass. Take 50 mg to 200 mg daily.
- Riboflavin helps maintain skin integrity and has also been used to treat migraines and sickle cell anemia. Take 10 mg to 20 mg daily.
- Niacin has anti-inflammatory properties, helps prevent diabetes and, in large dosages, lowers cholesterol. Take 100 mg to 200 mg daily.
- B5 plays an important role in energy production and in the manufacturing of certain hormones, and it may also help lower cholesterol. Take 10 mg to 200 mg daily.

- B6, one of the single most important nutrients to the human body, helps promote many enzymatic reactions in the body and is involved with communication between the nervous system and virtually every other part of your body. It is essential to optimal immune function and hormone balance. B6 is also used to treat depression, asthma, heart disease, peripheral nerve disease, premenstrual syndrome and carpal tunnel syndrome. Take 50 mg to 200 mg daily.
- Biotin maintains healthy hair and nails and may have some benefits for diabetics. Take 500 mcg to 5 mg daily.
- B12 is a critical element of proper heart function and lowers levels of homocysteine, an amino acid that appears to increase the risk of cardiovascular disease and dementia. B12 may actually help repair free radical damage to the central nervous system. Take 500 mcg to 5 mg a day, ideally in the methylcobalamin form.

If your multi vitamin doesn't contain these B-vitamins in these dosges, you can take a B-complex formulation, but be sure the formulation is properly balanced and includes folic acid (see below)

Folic acid

Folic acid is so important to brain health that, even though it is a B vitamin, it deserves a section of its own.

An exciting new Dutch study released in early 2007 shows that people between the ages of 50 and 70 who took 800 mcg of folic acid every day for three years significantly improved their scores on memory, information processing and sensory and motor coordination tests.

The same study showed that folic acid lowered homocysteine levels an average of 26 percent, dramatically lowering the risk of heart attack, stroke and memory impairment. Many studies show folic acid lowers blood pressure, reducing the risk for heart attacks and strokes.

And a large study from Tufts University connects high blood levels of folates and vitamin B12 with sharper memories in the elderly.

Perhaps most impressive is the 55 percent reduction in the risk of Alzheimer's in elderly people who got 3,400 mcg or more of folates daily reported in a 2004 University of California (Irvine) study.

Dosage: If you're over 50, take 800 mcg of folic acid every day without fail. That's how important I think this nutrient is. Always take B12 with folic acid to avoid masking a B12 deficiency.

Acetyl L-carnitine (ALCAR) and alpha lipoic acid (ALA)

There's no doubt in my mind that supplementation with these two nutrients can help improve memory and that they can reverse age-related cell damage that leads to memory loss and other diseases of aging.

Many scientists believe that as we age, our cells die because our mitochondria, which act like little furnaces producing energy for the body, fail to produce enough energy. It appears that acetyl L-carnitine (ALCAR) is a key nutrient for energy production at the cellular level to keep cells reproducing rather than deteriorating like a top winding down.

ALCAR is an amazing nutrient. There have been clinical trials showing that it can actually improve memory and cognitive functioning in patients already experiencing dementia.

In a recent study, patients with Alzheimer's disease undergoing standard drug therapy given two grams of ALCAR a day became more alert. Other research shows ALCAR slows memory loss in early onset dementia.

Alpha lipoic acid (ALA) is one of my favorite nutrients. It is a universal antioxidant because it has been shown to counteract the worst diseases of aging, including Alzheimer's, diabetes and heart disease. It helps de-activate an astonishing number of disease-causing free radicals. It's also a "green" antioxidant, because it helps recycle antioxidants such as vitamins C and E, helping prolong their disease-fighting capabilities.

ALA helps keep cell reproduction on track in a slightly different way than ALCAR. It has actually been shown to protect neurons and stop the formation of beta amyloid plaques that are part and parcel of Alzheimer's disease.

Animal studies show ALA actually helped regenerate brain cells and improve maze performance, and an Australian clinical study found that ALA slowed memory loss in patients with Alzheimer's.

But the real powerhouse antioxidant effect comes when you put ALCAR and ALA together. The two nutrients seem to act synergistically, each enhancing the power of the other.

Researchers at the University of Kentucky found that the two together were a potent force against some particularly nasty types of free radicals that target neurons and lead to dementia.

Combining the two nutrients made old rats act like young ones in studies by Dr. Bruce Ames of the University of California at Berkeley, one of the pioneers of antioxidant therapies. My experience shows me this may be true in humans as well, although there has not yet been any definitive research to prove it.

Dosage: If you are already experiencing memory loss, take 500 mg to 1,000 mg (1 gram) of ALCAR two or three times a day and 600 mg of ALA twice a day. If you are not experiencing memory loss and you're working to preserve your memory, lower dosages in the range of 500 mg of ALCAR and 150 mg of ALA are recommended.

Resveratrol

Found in red grapes, resveratrol has been called the immortality nutrient. It has been shown to give laboratory animals such long, healthy lives, that it would translate to an 11-year life extension if extrapolated to humans.

Certainly, the ancient Romans thought that drinking red wine daily would prolong their lives. They were right! You can get a good amount of resveratrol by drinking a glass of red wine every day, but there may be reasons why you don't want to do that. Good news! You can get the same effects in supplement form.

Each antioxidant has something unique about it, and reservatrol has two things that appeal to me:

First, it tricks your body into thinking it is on a low-calorie diet. Since loads of research shows that people and animals live longer if they eat very low-calorie diets and remain very thin, this is excellent news for those of us, like me, who love to eat, but want to stay thin.

Second, resveratrol seems to have an unusual ability to reduce inflammation. Recent research shows that chronic inflammation is an underlying cause of many disease conditions ranging from heart disease to cancer to lung disease, arthritis and diabetes and, you guessed it—Alzheimer's.

Resveratrol appears to work in the brain in several ways: it protects brain cells from destruction and deterioration; it reduces their demand for oxygen, which may be helpful during a stroke; it may persuade beta amyloid plaque cells to commit cellular suicide; and it protects the cellular DNA from being damaged.

Resveratrol has been shown to have the potential to protect brain cells and damage caused by strokes, control cholesterol, protect the kidneys and liver from aging and toxins, block cancer at virtually every stage of development, prevent blood clots, prevent damage to the heart muscle during a heart attack and block viruses, all at relatively low doses. It's not surprising that some experts are referring to it as the "cure-all" supplement.

Dosage: Take 50 mg to 300 mg a day.

Green tea

The Chinese and Japanese swear by it and their longevity and general good health are testimonials to a healthy diet and their love for this healthy leaf.

Green tea is packed with antioxidants, including the much-applauded polyphenol, epigallocatechin-3-gallate (EGCG), an anti-inflammatory compound that is well researched for its ability to stop free radical production and reduce the risk of heart disease, arthritis, cancer, degenerative neurological disease and many others.

In a study published in the *American Journal of Clinical Nutrition*, the value of drinking green tea was confirmed. More than 1,000 Japanese people, aged 70 and over, were questioned about their diets, overall health, lifestyle habits and frequency of green tea consumption. All study participants were tested for cognitive function to measure memory, attention and use of language. It was found that those with higher green tea consumption had a much lower risk for cognitive dysfunction. Those who drank two or more cups of green tea a day had about half the risk of developing some form of cognitive impairment compared to those who drank three cups or less per week. Study authors suggested that green tea's potential ability to support brain health may explain the lower rates of Alzheimer's disease in Japan compared to Europe and North America.

Citing just one of many examples from this body of literature, researchers adding EGCG to a culture of cancer cells were able to immediately stop further growth of these cancer cells. The lead researcher said that he was so impressed with the benefits of green tea that he began drinking it when the study results began to come in. It appears that the higher the dose of EGCG, the greater the effect.

In terms of protecting brain function, EGCG is actually considered a unique free radical scavenger because it seems to single out neurons that are being attacked by Alzheimer's and other forms of dementia and protect them from further deterioration.

L-theanine, an important amino acid found in green tea, also works to protect neurons and to enhance the brain's natural production of neurotransmitters that are disrupted in AD and dementia. Animal studies show L-theanine helps improve memory and learning abilities.

Green tea may also protect against permanent brain damage after strokes and head injuries.

That means you can sit and drink green tea all day long and be happy and healthy for the experience!

Dosage: Drink as many cups of green tea as you like, but if that's not your cup of tea, take 50 mg to 500 mg of standardized green tea extract. If you're also trying to lose weight, take 500 mg to 1,000 mg daily.

Aged garlic extract

Aged garlic extract, best known for its heart-protective and immune-system-enhancing effects, takes its substantial health benefits a step further to protect brain function.

It almost sounds like this humble little bulb is a Samurai warrior, attacking four specific free radical molecules that contribute to loss of brain function and stopping the inflammation that contributes to the formation of the beta amyloid plaques characteristic of Alzheimer's and other forms of dementia.

Garlic also helps with the learning process and the ability to retain information over a long period of time, according to Japanese research.

Garlic is composed of a large number of nutrients, all of which enhance the others, so it's a good idea to get your garlic as plain old garlic in your food.

You can eat your garlic raw or cooked without losing nutrients. For those who prefer to keep their friends (the odor comes from the sulfur compounds), aged garlic extract is the way to go. Not only does it help preserve your social status, most of the research is done on these odorless products and they are effective.

Dosage: Take 600 mg to 1,200 mg daily.

Other great brain protectors

Antioxidants have a shotgun effect to help keep your body and brain young, but there are several very effective supplements that are laser-like in their ability to keep brain cells healthy and to target failing brain cells and give them a boost:

Ginkgo biloba

Ginkgo may be one of the best known supplements for cognitive decline, partly because it is a triple threat. Clinical trials have shown ginkgo:

- May help healthy people improve their memories
- Can improve memory in people with failing memories
- Can slow the decline for those diagnosed with AD

Ginkgo extract has been used extensively and successfully in Europe to relieve symptoms of a variety of cognitive problems. In a 1997 study reported in the prestigious *Journal of the American Medical Association*, people diagnosed with Alzheimer's or dementia took 120 mg of a special ginkgo extract called Egb761 for one year. Of those participants, 27 percent made a substantial improvement in memory and social skills and 37 percent made at least some improvement.

A British study compared ginkgo, glucose and pure oxygen for improving mental sharpness. Researchers first gave college students a sugary drink containing 25 grams of glucose, while other students drank a placebo, and then followed this by doing a series of calculations. The students given the glucose had a clear improvement in their ability to calculate over a period of a few minutes.

In another experiment using oxygen, students were able to memorize two or three more words out of a list of 15 compared to those not using oxygen.

Finally, ginkgo was tested and it was found that students given ginkgo improved their memories for up to six hours compared to a benefit of only a few minutes with the intake of pure oxygen or glucose.

Other research has suggested ginkgo may be at least as effective as Aricept, the popular prescription drug used to treat AD.

Scientists think part of ginkgo's magic comes from its ability to improve circulation throughout the body and especially to the brain.

However, the research on memory in healthy people is mixed. The U.S. government thinks ginkgo is important enough that it is conducting a large study at several sites across the country. We won't know the results for a few more years.

Dosage: Take 120 mg to 360 mg of ginkgo (standardized to contain six percent terpene lactones and 24 percent flavone glycosides) per day, generally divided into two or three portions. You need to take ginkgo for eight to 12 weeks before you notice improvement. Ginkgo has been shown to increase bleeding, so you should stop take it if you are planning to have surgery and you should not take it at all if you are taking Coumadin or other blood thinners.

Phosphatidylserine (PS)

On February 24, 2003, the Food and Drug Administration (FDA) allowed two health claims for a nutrient called phosphatidylserine (PS). The first claim is that PS may reduce the risk of cognitive dysfunction in the elderly, and the second claim is that PS may reduce the risk of dementia in the elderly.

As a neurologist who treats patients with Alzheimer's and dementia on a daily basis, I was certainly pleased to see this.

These health claims approved by the FDA should not be taken lightly. The issue underwent several months of review of the medical literature before the claims were approved. Bear in mind that most vitamins and nutrients sold do not carry any FDA health claims. Products must meet the FDA's requirements that they are safe and lawful at the levels needed to justify a health claim.

Phosphatidylserine (PS) belongs to a special category of fat-soluble substances called phospholipids, which are essential components of cell membranes. PS is related to lecithin, a naturally occurring compound found in high concentrations in the brain.

In people with Alzheimer's, PS has been shown to improve mental function, such as the ability to remember names and to recall the location of misplaced objects.

PS is one of the few nutrients that may be helpful for people with advanced Alzheimer's. In one double-blind trial, only the most seriously impaired participants received benefits from taking PS; people with moderate AD did not experience significant improvements in cognitive function.

Scientists speculate that PS encourages the regrowth of damaged nerve networks.

Based on the blessing from the FDA, I now recommend this nutrient to many of my senior patients with declining memory and dementia. It helps some and doesn't help others, but it's worth it considering the possible benefits.

Dosage: Take 300 mg to 600 mg of PS in divided doses daily.

Vinpocetine

Vinpocetine comes from the leaves of Vinca minor, also known as lesser periwinkle.

This plant extract has several unique effects including:
• Increasing blood circulation in the brain
• Increasing brain metabolism
• Possibly reducing the loss of neurons due to decreased blood flow.

In three studies of older adults with memory problems associated with poor brain circulation or dementia-related disease, vinpocetine produced more improvement than a placebo in performance on global cognitive tests reflecting attention, concentration and memory.

A wide variety of studies suggest that vinpocetine can help with memory retention and may improve mild memory loss.

Studies show it doesn't have any real effect on Alzheimer's patients.

Vinpocetine is most effective in people who have who have inadequate blood flow to their brains since it dilates the blood vessels.

Dosage: Take 30 mg to 60 mg of vinpocetine daily. Taking it with food appears to dramatically improve its absorption.

Melatonin

Melatonin is a natural hormone that regulates the human biological clock. Night workers, truck drivers and people with jet lag often find melatonin helps them re-balance their body clocks.

Since melatonin is responsible for regulating the sleep-wake cycles, and good brain function is closely linked to proper sleep patterns, it stands to reason that melatonin would be effective in keeping cognitive function on track.

It turns out that melatonin does that and more. This little hormone is a powerful anti-inflammatory that may help protect neurons and stop the formation of the beta-amyloid plaques characteristic of Alzheimer's, and Chinese research suggests it is helpful in enhancing learning capabilities.

Natural melatonin levels decrease as we age and people with Alzheimer's tend to have the lowest levels of melatonin. Taking melatonin supplements appears to possibly slow the progress of mild Alzheimer's.

Melatonin may also be helpful to people with diabetes who are at high risk for AD and dementia. Turkish research shows that melatonin supplements can help slow cognitive impairment and improve learning abilities.

Dosage: Take 3 mg to 10 mg daily, starting with a lower dosage and only increasing it if you don't see effects after three months.

SAM-e (S-adenosylmethionine) and TMG (trimethylglycine)

S-adenosylmethionine (SAM-e) helps in the production of several brain chemicals that improve mood, energy, well-being, alertness, concentration and visual clarity. Trimethylglycine (TMG, also known as betaine) helps your body produce SAM-e naturally and is often called the "poor man's SAM-e" because of its considerably lower price.

SAM-e has gained favor in recent years as an effective treatment for mild to moderate depression.

Both SAM-e and TMG belong to a group of nutrients called methyl donors that help neutralize the brain-damaging effects of homocysteine.

Homocysteine contributes to increased risk of heart disease and strokes. It is also a neurotoxin and an underlying factor in AD and dementia. That's why high homocysteine levels increase the risk of AD.

In addition to its ability to help produce the neurotransmitters needed to create a healthy mood and proper brain function, SAM-e has been shown to protect neurons by slowing the production of beta amyloid proteins that result in the formation of the plaques characteristic of AD.

Canadian researchers found that SAM-e levels were as much as 85 percent lower in elderly people with AD than in those with no cognitive impairment. That's a very impressive number that makes a strong suggestion that keeping SAM-e levels high may offer some protective effect.

One study from Baylor University even suggests that intravenous or oral administration of SAM-e might be a treatment for Alzheimer's.

Dosage: Start with 400 mg a day and if you don't see effects after several weeks, go up to 800 mg to 1,600 mg.

Turmeric (curcumin)

This tasty, bright-yellow spice that gives curry its flavor and color has been shown in laboratory and animal studies to actually stop the growth of beta-amyloid plaques that are characteristic of AD and to stop the clumping and tangling of fibers that disrupt the memory pathways. One animal study actually shows that curcumin, the active ingredient in turmeric, actually reduced the number of plaques and tangles. Turmeric's value may help explain the low rate of Alzheimer's in India where curried foods are a dietary staple.

Dosage: Turmeric comes in capsules or as a spice. If you're taking it in capsule form, take 400 mg to 1,000 mg three times per day; or 0.5 gram to 1 gram of powdered root, up to 3 grams per day.

NADH (nicotinamide adenine dinucleotide)

This coenzyme form of the B vitamin, niacin, is specially activated and actually helps cells extract energy from food sources.

Japanese researchers found that people with Alzheimer's have lower blood levels of NADH.

Dr. Stanley Cohan of the Georgetown University Research Medical Center is director of a program studying NADH to treat Alzheimer's disease. This is what he says:

- Currently proven treatments and therapies for people with Alzheimer's disease are inadequate.
- NADH is a naturally occurring compound (a coenzyme) with few side effects that has shown promise in Europe and is in preliminary trials with Alzheimer's disease patients.

Considering the shortage of effective ways to treat Alzheimer's, it's certainly worth a try.

Dosage: 10 mg to 20 mg daily

Huperzine

Huperzia is a type of moss that grows in China. Modern herbal preparations use only an isolated component known as huperzine A.

Huperzine A is an alkaloid that prevents the breakdown of acetylcholine, an important substance needed by the nervous system to transmit information from cell to cell. Animal research has suggested that huperzine A may work better than some prescription drugs to preserve acetylcholine.

Loss of acetylcholine function is a major risk in AD. Huperzine A may also have a protective effect on brain tissue, further increasing its theoretical potential for helping reduce symptoms of some brain disorders.

In a Chinese study, more than half the people with Alzheimer's disease tested had significant improvement in memory and cognitive and behavioral functions after taking 200 mcg of huperzine A twice per day for eight weeks. Another study using injected huperzine A confirmed a positive effect in people with dementia, including, but not limited to, Alzheimer's disease. A third study found that huperzine A (100–150 mcg two to three times per day for four to six weeks) was more effective for improving minor memory loss than the drug piracetam (brand name: Nootropil®, Myocalm®).

Huperzine A is also helpful in memory and learning in young people.

One small controlled study of middle school students found that 100 mcg of huperzine A two times per day for four weeks was effective in improving memory and learning performance.

Dosage: Take 200 mcg to 400 mcg daily.

References:

Frank B, Gupta S. *A review of antioxidants and Alzheimer's disease. Annals of Clinical Psychiatry* 2005 Oct-Dec;17(4):269-86.

Freund-Levi Y Eriksdotter-Jönhagen M et al. *N-3 Fatty acid treatment in 174 patients with mild to moderate Alzheimer disease: OmegAD Study: a randomized double-blind trial. Archives of Neurology* 2006;63:1402-1408.

Schaefer E, Bongard V et al. *Plasma phosphatidylcholine docosahexaenoic acid content and risk of dementia and Alzheimer disease: the Framingham Heart Study. Archives of Neurology* 2006;63:1545-1550.

Nantz, M, Rowe C et al. *Immunity and antioxidant capacity in humans is enhanced by consumption of a dried, encapsulated fruit and vegetable Juice Concentrate. Journal of Nutrition* 2006; 136:2606-2610.

Lucotti P, Setola E et al. *Beneficial effects of a long-term oral L-arginine treatment added to a hypocaloric diet and exercise training program in obese, insulin-resistant type 2 diabetic patients. American Journal of Physiology, Endocrinology and Metabolism* 2006;291:E906-E912.

Haan MN, Miller JW et al. *Homocysteine, B vitamins and the incidence of dementia and cognitive impairment: results from the Sacramento Area Latino Study on Aging. American Journal of Clinical Nutrition* 2007; 85(2):511-7.

Durga J, van Boxtel MP et al. *Effect of 3-year folic acid supplementation in older adults in the FACIT trial: a randomized, double blind, controlled trial. Lancet* 2007 Jan 20;369(9557):203-16.

Fleng L, Ng TP et al. *Homocysteine, folate and vitamin B-12 and cognitive performance in older Chinese adults: findings from the Singpaore Longitudinal Aging Study. American Journal of Clinical Nutrition* 2006 Dec;84(6):1506-12.

Morris MS, Jacques PF et al. *Folate and vitamin B012 status in relation to anemia, macrocytosis and cognitive impairment in older Americans in the age of folic acid fortification. American Journal of Clinical Nutrition* 2007;85(1):193-200.

Corrada, M et al. *Alzheimer's and dementia. Journal of the Alzheimer's Association* July 2005;1(1);11-18.

Holmquist L, Stuchbury G et al. *Lipoic acid as a novel treatment for Alzheimer's disease and related dementias. Pharmacology and Therapeutics* 2007 Jan;113(1);154-64.

De Arriba SG, Loske C et al. *Advanced glycation end products induce changes in glucose consumption, lactate production and ATP levels in SH-SY5Y neuroblastoma cells by a redox-sensitive mechanism. Journal of Cerebral Blood Flow and Metabolism* 2003 Nov;23(11):1307-13.

Abdul HM, Butterfield DA. *Involvement of PI3K/PKG/ERK1/2 signaling pathways in cortical neurons to trigger protection by co treatment of acetyl-L-carnitine and alpha lipoic acid against HNE-mediated oxidative stress and neurotoxicity: implications for Alzheimer's disease. Free Radical Biology and Medicine* 2007;42(3):371-84.

Baur J, Pearson K et al. *Resveratrol improves health and survival of mice on a high-calorie diet. Nature.* 2006 Nov 16;444(7117):337-42.

Hall SS. *Longevity research. In vino vitalis? Compounds activate life-extending research. Science* 2003 Aug 29;301(5637)1165.

De la Lastra CA, Vollegas I. *Resveratrol as an anti-inflammatory and anti-aging agent: mechanisms and clinical implications. Molecular Nutrition and Food Research* 2005 May;49(5):405-30.

Zilka N, Ferencik M et al. *Neuroinflammation in Alzheimer's disease: protector or promoter? Bratislavské lekárske listy* 2006;107(9-10):374-83.

Zini R, Morin C et al. *Effects of Resveratrol on the rat brain respiratory chain. Drugs Expo Clinical Research* 1999;25:87-97.

Zini R, Morin C et al. *Resveratrol-induced limitation of dysfunction of mitochondria isolated form rat brain in an anoxia-reoxygenated model. Life Sciences* 2002;71;3091-108.

Jan JH, Surh YJ. *Protective effect of Resveratrol on beta-amyloid-induced oxidative PC 12 cell death. Free Radical Biology and Medicine* 2003:34;1100-10.

Russo A, Palumbo M et al. *Red wine micronutrients as protective agents in Alzheimer-like induced insult. Life Sciences* 2003:72;2369-79.

Shinichi K, Atsushi H et al. *Green tea consumption and cognitive function: a cross-sectional study from the Tsurugaya Project. American Journal of Clinical Nutrition,* Feb 2006;83:355-361.

Kostrzewa RM, Segura-Aguilar J. *Novel mechanisms and approaches in the study of neurodegeneration and neuroprotection. A review. Neurotoxicity Research* 2003;5(6):375-83.

Nathan PJ, Lu K et al. The neuropharmacology of L-theanine (N-ethyl-L-glutamine): a possible neuroprotective and cognitive enhancing agent. Journal of Herbal Pharmacotherapy 2006:6(2):21-30.

Kakuda T, Neuroprotective effects of the green tea components theanine and catechins. Biological and Pharmaceutical Bulletin 2002 Dec;25(12):1513-8.

Choi YB, Kim YI et al. Protective effect of epigallocatechin gallate on brain damage after transient middle cerebral artery occlusion in rats. Brain Research 2004 Sep 3;1019(1-2):47-54.

Borek C. Garlic reduces dementia and heart-disease risk. Journal of Nutrition 2006 Mar;136(3 Supl):810S-812S.

Borek C. Antioxidant health effects of aged garlic extract. Journal of Nutrition 2001 Mar;131(3s):1010-5S.

Moriguchi T, Takashina K. Prolongation of life span and improved learning in the senescence accelerated mouse produced by aged garlic extract. Biological and Pharmaceutical Bulletin 17(12):1589-94.

Gao S, Jin Y et al. Selenium level and cognitive function in rural elderly Chinese. American Journal of Epidemiology 2007 Apr 15;165(8):955-65.

Le Bars PL. Magnitude of effect and special approach to Ginkgo biloba extract EGb 761 in cognitive disorders. Pharmapsychiatry 2003 Jun;36 Suppl 1:S44-9.

Freedman AM, Schatzberg AF. A placebo-controlled, double-blind, randomized trial of an extract of Ginkgo biloba for dementia. North American EGb Study Group. Journal of the American Medical Association 1997;278:1327-1332.

Crook T, Petrie W et al. Effects of phosphatidylserine in Alzheimer's disease. Psychopharmacology Bulletin 1992;28:61-6.

Amaducci L. Phosphatidylserine in the treatment of Alzheimer's disease: results of a multicenter study. Psychopharmacology Bulletin 1988;24:130-4.

Furushiro M, Suzuki S et al. Effects of oral administration of soybean lecithin transphosphatidylated phosphatidylserine on impaired learning of passive avoidance in mice. Japanese Journal of Pharmacology 1997;75:447-50.

Sakai M, Yamatoya H et al. Pharmacological effects of phosphatidylserine enzymatically synthesized from soybean lecithin on brain functions in rodents. Journal of Nutritional Sciences and Vitaminology (Tokyo) 1996;42:47-54.

Blokland A, Honig W et al. Cognition-enhancing properties of subchronic phosphatidylserine (PS) treatment in middle-aged rats: comparison of bovine cortex PS with egg PS and soybean PS. Nutrition 1999;15:778-83.

McDaniel MA, Maier SF et al. "Brain-specific" nutrients: a memory cure? Nutrition 2003 Nov-Dec;19(11-12):957-75.

Horvath S. The use of vinpocetine in chronic disorders caused by cerebral hypoperfusion. Orvosi Hetilap 2001 Feb 25;142(8):383-9.

Kemeny V, Molnar S et al. Acute and chronic effects of vinpocetine on cerebral hemodynamics and neuropsychological performance in multi-infarct patients. Journal of Clinical Pharmacology 2005 Sep;45(9):1048-54.

Vas A, Christer H et al. Human positron tomography with oral 11C-vinpocetine. Orvosi Hetilap 2003 Nov 16;144(46):2271-6.

Lohmann A, Dingler E et al. Bioavailability of vinpocetine and interference of the time of application with food intake. Arzneimittelforschung 1992;42:914-7.

Hindmarch I, Fuchs HH et al. Efficacy and tolerance of vinpocetine in ambulant patients suffering from mild to moderate organic psychosyndromes. International Clinical Psychopharmacology 1991;6:31-43.

Shen Y, Zhang G et al. Suppressive effects of melatonin on amyloid-beta-induced glial activation in rat hippocampus. Archives of Medical Research 2007 Apr;38(3):284-90.

Wang JZ, Wang ZF. Role of melatonin in Alzheimer-like neurodegeneration. Acta pharmacologica Sinica 2006 Jan;27(1):41-9.

Tuzcu M, Baydas G. Effects of melatonin and vitamin E on diabetes-induced learning and memory impairment in rats. European Journal of Pharmacology 2006 May 10;537(1-3):106-10.

Scarpa S, Cavalarro RA et al. Gene silencing through methylation: an epigenetic intervention on Alzheimer disease. Journal of Alzheimer's Disease 2006 Aug;9(4):407-14.

Fuso A, Seminara L. S-adenosylmethionine/homocysteine cycle alterations modify DNA methylation status with consequent deregulation of PS1 and BACE and beta-amyloid production. Molecular and Cellular Neurosciences 2005 Jan;28(1):195-204.

Knopman D, Patterson M. An open-label, 24-week pilot study of the methyl donor betaine in Alzheimer disease patients. Alzheimer Disease and Associated Disorders 2001 Jul-Sep;15(3):162-5.

Morrison LD, Smith DD et al. Brain S-adenosylmethionine levels are severely decreased in Alzheimer's disease. Journal of Neurochemistry 1996 Sep;67(3):1328-31.

Bottiglieri T, Myland K. S-adenosylmethionine levels in psychiatric and neurological disorders: a review. Acta neurological Scandinavica (Supp) 1994;154:19-26.

Cheng DH, Tang XC. Comparative studies of huperzine A, E2020, and tacrine on behavior and cholinesterase activities. Pharmacology, Biochemistry and Behavior 1998;60:377-86.

Yang F, Lim GP et al. Curcumin inhibits formation of amyloid beta oligometers and fibrils, binds plaques and reduces amyloid in vivo. Journal of Biological Chemistry 2005 Feb 18;280(7):5892-901.

Garcia-Alloza M, Borelli LA et al. Curcumin labels amyloid pathology in vivo, disrupts existing plaques and partially restores distorted neurites in an Alzheimer mouse model. Journal of Neurochemistry 2007 Apr 30; (Epub ahead of print).

Cheng DH, Ren H et al. Huperzine A, a novel promising acetylcholinesterase inhibitor. Neuroreport 1996;8:97–101.

Ved HS, Koenig ML et al. Huperzine A, a potential therapeutic agent for dementia, reduces neuronal cell death caused by glutamate. Neuroreport 1997;8:963–8.

Skolnick AA. Old Chinese herbal medicine used for fever yields possible new Alzheimer's disease therapy [news item]. Journal of the American Medical Association 1997;277:776.

Xu SS, Gao ZX et al. Efficacy of tablet huperzine-A on memory, cognition, and behavior in Alzheimer's disease. Chung Kuo Yao Li Hsueh Pao 1995;16:391–5.

Zhang RW, Tang XC et al. Drug evaluation of huperzine A in the treatment of senile memory disorders. Chung Kuo Yao Li Hsueh Pao 1991;12:250–2.

Wang Z, Ren G, et al. A double-blind study of huperzine A and piracetam in patients with age-associated memory impairment and dementia. In: Kanba S, Richelson E (eds). Herbal Medicines for Nonpsychiatric Diseases. Tokyo: Seiwa Shoten Publishers, 1999;39–50.

Nakamura S, Kawamata T, Reduced nicotinamide adenine dinucleopeptide diaphorase histochemistry in neocortex and hippocampus with Alzheimer type dementia and aged controls. Rinsho Shinkeigaku 1987 Aug;27(8):1059-63.

Kidd PM, Neurodegeneration from mitochondrial insufficiency: nutrients, stem cells, growth factors and prospects for brain rebuilding using integrative management. Alternative Medicine Review 2005 Dec;10(4):268-93.

Conclusion

Alzheimer's and other types of dementia are unlike other chronic degenerative diseases. There is no cure. There is no really effective treatment, although there are some treatments that can delay the onset or slow the mental deterioration.

With heart disease, a bypass will end the problem for years. With cancer, chemotherapy or radiation may even bring about a cure. There are many supplements that can help reverse the symptoms of both deadly diseases.

It is my greatest frustration that, as a doctor, I cannot offer the families of people with Alzheimer's or dementia any real hope based on medical science as we know it today.

The human brain is unforgiving. I know, I said earlier in this book that the human brain is plastic and capable of learning throughout life. While this is basically true and the human brain is changeable and adaptable, it is very rigid compared to the body's other organ systems. When things start to go wrong in the brain, it's a downhill slide. The pace of that slide may be slowed, but the outcome is inevitable.

Even though the brain can expand and learn and repair itself throughout life, we all know that a brain injury to an eight-year-old is very different from a brain injury in an 80-year-old. The eight-year-old may be able to adapt and forge new neural pathways and regain brain function that has been lost; the 80-year-old brain is unlikely to regain what has been lost.

You may be reading this book because you are the child or the grandchild of someone with AD or dementia. I know you are looking for hope and it is my greatest sorrow that I cannot offer that to you.

ROLE REVERSAL

If you are fortunate to have your parents or grandparents live long enough, there comes a time when the roles reverse and the child becomes the parent. It may begin subtly and it may not even have any great bearing on cognitive function. It may begin with Mom wanting your advice on her investments or Dad asking you to help research what kind of car to buy. This is a pivotal point in parent-child relationships and a payback for all their love and caring that I wish I had been able to offer to my parents, who are no longer with us.

If you have a parent or grandparent with cognitive impairment, now is the time for you to help them walk. They held your hand as you took your first steps. Now it is your turn to hold their hands as they take their last ones. It is part of the circle of life and it is indeed a sacred task.

Someone you love is slipping away and there is little you or I can do about it, except perhaps soften the long goodbye.

In time, you'll have to make that heart-wrenching decision to let professionals take care of them when it becomes physically, emotionally and mentally impossible for you to do so.

TAKE CARE OF YOURSELF

Your loved one is not reading this book. You are. Perhaps the only good thing about AD is that people with the disease seem to be blissfully unaware of the chaos taking place in their brains.

You're reading this book because you care. Of course, you care about your loved one, but you need to care for yourself, too. As a caregiver, you must make yourself a priority so you can be there when Mom or Dad and Grandma or Grandpa need you. You also need to be there for yourself and your spouse and children.

I can offer you here the take-home message that will change your life:

Don't wait for the other shoe to drop. Start now. Today. Save your own brain and preserve your own future. Use it or lose it.

I can't say it any more clearly: If you are at high risk for AD or other forms of dementia, you need to make the choice to start your brain training program today. Even if your risk isn't particularly high, what you do today will make your brain stronger and sharper tomorrow and for years down the road.

It doesn't matter how old you are. You're younger today than you will be tomorrow. Start today. Do everything you can to keep your memory intact.

In this book, I've talked to you at length about the importance of diet, exercise, lifestyle and supplements. These are important, but they're important for general healthy living.

What's different here is the mental conditioning part of this program. Without it, nothing else will work.

When you're tired from a long day of work or worse yet, a long day of taking care of Grandma, remember this: Your ability to keep your mind functional, sharp and clear depends almost completely on your willingness to challenge it and keep it strong throughout your life.

So get out that sudoku book, grab the crossword, sign up for that Spanish class or join a line dancing club. It will, quite literally, save your life.